Online Course Mastery: The Ultimate Guide to Creating and Marketing Profitable Online Courses

Learn How to Find Your Niche, Create Engaging Content, and Succeed as an Online Course Creator.

Change Your Life Guru

Books by **Change Your Life Guru**:

Affiliate Marketing Mastery: *The Ultimate Guide to Starting Your Online Business and Earning Passive Income - Unlock Profitable Affiliate Secrets, Boost Earnings with Expert Strategies, Top Niches, High-Performance Products, Innovative Tactics and Essential Tools for Success*

Dropshipping Business Mastery: *The Ultimate Guide to Starting & Managing a Thriving Dropshipping Business - Skyrocket Your Income with Proven Strategies, Profitable Niches, and Unleash Powerful Marketing Tactics*

Etsy Store Mastery: *The Ultimate Guide to Building Your Own Etsy Empire - Learn Proven Strategies for Finding & Selling the Hottest Products, Building Your Brand, and Dominating Your Niche on Etsy*

Online Course Mastery: *The Ultimate Guide to Creating and Marketing Profitable Online Courses - Learn How to Find Your Niche, Create Engaging Content, and Succeed as an Online Course Creator*

Online Freelancing Mastery: *The Ultimate Guide to Making Money as an Online Freelancer - Unlock Proven Strategies to Monetize Your Skills and Talents, Market Yourself, and Go from Zero To Success*

Online Tutoring: *The Ultimate Guide to Creating a Profitable Online Tutoring Business – Become an Expert in Your Niche, Craft Engaging Sessions, Harness Powerful Marketing Strategies, and Profit from Your Expertise in the Digital Learning World*

Print on Demand Mastery: *The Ultimate Blueprint for Print on Demand Success - Unlock Actionable Tips & Strategies to Starting, Setting Up, and Marketing a Profitable Print on Demand Business*

Social Media Influencer: *The Ultimate Guide to Building a Profitable Social Media Influencer Career - Learn How to Build Your Brand, Create Viral Content, and Make Brands Beg to Pay for Your Lifestyle*

Subscription Business Model: *The Ultimate Guide to Building and Scaling A Predictable Recurring Income Business - Attract and Retain Loyal Subscribers, and Maximize Your Profitability with Proven Strategies and Best Practices*

YouTube Influencer: *The Ultimate Guide to YouTube Success, Content Creation, and Monetization Strategies - Build and Grow a Thriving YouTube Channel and Boost Engagement with Proven Techniques and Insider Secrets*

THANK YOU – A Gift For You!

THANK YOU for purchasing our book! *You could have chosen from dozens of other books on the same topic but you took a chance and chose this one.* As a token of our appreciation, we would like to offer you an exclusive **FREE GIFT BOX**. Your Gift Box contains powerful downloadable products, resources and tools that are the perfect companion to your newly-acquired book, and are designed to catapult you towards freedom and success.

To get instant access, just go to:
https://changeyourlife.guru/toolkit

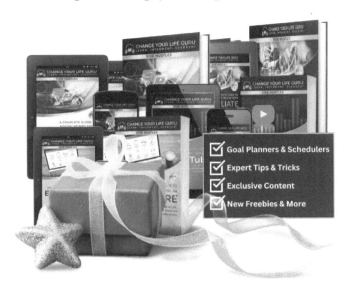

Inside your Free Gift Box, you'll receive:

- **Goal Planners and Schedulers**: Map out manageable and actionable steps so you have clarity and are empowered with a clear roadmap to achieve every goal.

- **Expert Tips & Tricks:** Invaluable tips and strategies ready to apply to your life, or business, to accelerate your progress and reach your outcomes.

- **Exclusive Content:** Free bonus materials, resources, and tools to help you succeed.

- **New Freebies:** Enter your email address to download your free gift box and be updated when we add new Free Content, ensuring you always have the tools, information and strategies to sky-rocket your success!

Are you ready to supercharge your life? Download your gift box for FREE today! [**https://changeyourlife.guru/toolkit**]

Table of Contents

Introduction

The only way to get started is to quit talking and begin doing. -
Walt Disney

Though online courses have been around for a long time, it was not until 2020 that they really became popular. As lockdowns came into play—and stayed in place for quite a while—and work from home situations became more and more popular, new methods of learning and teaching were adopted by a myriad of different people. From university and colleges, to private tutors and to personal trainers. Suddenly it seemed like everyone was offering an online course of some sort. Well, everyone who had something to teach to others, that is. This was only to be expected though, considering the numerous, nearly countless benefits that online courses offer to both students and instructors. For students, the benefits range from having the freedom to learn any and all subjects, being able to learn at your own, unique pace, and to having their disabilities be accounted for as they learn, making the entire process easier for them. Of course, there are also the comforts of learning from home and the opportunities students get to develop their various technical skills as they learn.

Though online courses have many benefits for students, they have even more for instructors or inspiring instructors such as yourself. For one, instructors have access to a greater variety of teaching tools when teaching online courses. For another, they are able to save a great deal of time and be more flexible with their own time. They also are able to work from the comfort of their own homes, increase their students' access to their instructors, reduce the amount of administrative work that they have to do, have a much easier time updating course content and making it accessible to their pupils and maintain thorough records of classes and lessons. Then there is the very simple fact that online courses give instructors the opportunity to earn a good, steady income for years and years, with minimal work. So long as the quality of the work—that is to say, the course material and teaching—is high, instructors can earn a great deal of money through courses they only have to create once.

With all this being the case, it should be no surprise that online courses have become a bit of a global trend. Except, unlike most trends, they are here to stay. Take the online learning platform, Coursera, for instance. Coursera was founded in 2012, meaning it has been around for a good 11 years up to this point. But it was not until 2020-2021 that it experienced a genuine boom. In 2021 alone the platform, which partners with universities, colleges, and companies to deliver online learning to their customers, gained 20 million new student registrations. In 2020, Coursera had a grand total of 71 million users. By 2021, that figure had risen to 91 million. The same kind of thing happened with course enrollments on the platform. Once lockdowns went into effect and work from home became the norm, those enrollments increased by about 32%. Of course, Coursera was by no means the only platform to benefit from the situation in this way. Other platforms like Udemy, Lynda, Skillshare, and Udacity suddenly found themselves catering to millions of students as well. That each of these platforms catered to different kinds of students and offered them different learning opportunities played a part in this. Coursera, for instance, delivers more academic education to e-learners. Skillshare, on the other hand, delivers courses and training to creative individuals seeking to improve their skills, like photography or animation.

Since 2020, these different platforms have only improved and students have steadily continued signing up for different courses and they will continue to do so for a long time to come. What that means is that teaching online courses is a viable and very lucrative way of earning an income and will be just that for the foreseeable future. The online courses market, which was worth about $190 billion dollars in 2015 is projected to be worth $319 billion dollars in 2029. That is a pretty massive pie and you too can have a slice of it, if you know how to create quality online courses and market them well. For context, a successful online course can make you between $1-$10k per month. How much you earn will depend on things like how you price your courses, how you do marketing and social media marketing, and whether you are able to build a community around the course you are teaching. All that might sound like a bit of a tall order. However, it is very doable, so long as you know the right way to go about crafting your own online course and getting the word out about it. This is why the most successful online course creators earn six to seven-figure incomes per year.

So, how do you go about creating a successful online course? What makes a successful course anyways? Which platforms should you use for what you want to teach and how do you use them? What skills do you need to be able to create online courses and how are you supposed to market your online course anyways? *A Complete Guide to Creating Online Courses* answers all of these questions and more. In doing so, it shows you how to create the perfect course for you to teach. It also shows you how to prepare the perfect, quality course materials that could make your course's stellar reputation and shows you how to go about getting the word out about your work. It walks you through each of the steps you need to take to make your course a roaring success and establish you as a true expert in your field. So, without further ado, are you ready to begin?

Chapter 1:
Finding Your Niche

You might think that the first step to starting an online course is deciding on what platform you want and figuring out how to navigate it. However, the process of starting an online course begins much sooner than that. It begins with figuring out what your specific niche is and how it fits into the existing marketplace.

To start, what exactly is a niche and why does it matter? A niche is the segment of a market—any market, not just online teaching—that is defined by its own unique needs and preferences. Think of a niche like it were a slice of a big cake. This slice is meant for people who have specific needs, interests, or wants. It's chocolate flavored for people who like chocolate but dairy–free for people who are lactose intolerant. Online knitting classes, for instance, might be a good example of a niche in this specific market. Home workouts or yoga classes, experienced a huge boom during the lockdown phase of the pandemic. The same can be said of English tutoring sessions for high school students studying to take the TOEFL or online cooking classes for beginners.

Finding your niche in the online courses industry is extremely important. Your niche is what sets you apart from all the other online instructors out there, after all. It is what draws a specific audience to you and it is even something that plays a part in your holding onto a solid audience base. So, how can you go about finding your niche? In other words, what do you need to do to cut out a slice that is yours and yours alone of the online courses pie?

How to Find Your Niche

Finding your very own niche requires some degree of reflection. First, you need to reflect on what your interests, passions, and expertise are. Is there a hobby or skill that you are particularly good at? Is there a field or area, like American history or mindful meditation techniques, that you have a wealth of knowledge on? Is there a topic that you would feel comfortable and feel confident teaching others about? These are the kinds of things you will need to reflect on when you are first trying to uncover your niche. Sometimes, though, the answers to these questions might not be all that obvious. You might struggle with coming up with a field or skill that you think you are good enough to teach others. Alternatively, you might not be all that confident that you have a firm enough grasp of your topic to be able to communicate it to others. All of that is perfectly understandable. Luckily, you can overcome such confusion, uncertainty, and double by asking yourself a set of questions. The answers you honestly give to these questions can then help you to pinpoint your expertise, skills, and passions more easily:

- Are there any skills that come naturally to me? If so, what are they?

- What topics and subtopics do I enjoy learning about the most?

- How do I like spending my free time?

- What kind of problems am I able to solve?

- Are there any subjects that my friends, colleagues, or family members usually request my expertise on?

- Who do I want to help and how can I help them?

You might think that things like your passions or interests might not matter as much within the context of online courses. You would, however, be wrong. Your passions and interests are things that you can communicate to your audience with ease and eagerness. They are tools, in a sense, that you can use to get them as excited about that subject as you are. The excitement you feel when talking about such subjects you are interested in is something that will be reflected in your gestures, mimics, and tone of voice. It is something that will similarly be reflected in how you talk about and discuss the subject in question. Your passions and interests, then, are things that can help you to affect how engaged your audience is in the class or course you are teaching.

An engaged student, after all, is one who will keep coming back to your lessons again and again.

Identify Your Students and Their Needs

It is important that you do not just answer these questions in your mind. Instead, you should write your answers down on one page of a notebook. This will make the next step of the process a bit easier to tackle. This next step is to identify your future students' needs and problems. What needs do they have that they want met? What problems are they having that they want solved? In other words, what would motivate prospective students to try your courses? To figure these things out, you can again ask yourself a set of questions and write down their answer on the opposite page of your notebook :

- Who are my potential learners?

- What do they like and what do they dislike?

- What specific set of skills do they need or want to learn?

- What are they looking for?

By asking yourself these questions, you will have gained a clearer picture of who your target audience is. However, there are things you can do to clarify that picture even more. You can, for instance, have one-on-one conversations with members of your target market, so that you can truly begin to see what it is they are looking for. Such conversations can help you to become aware of the struggles they face in their efforts to learn the subjects they want to learn. In discovering these struggles, you can devise and construct your online courses so that they overcome those struggles and obstacles. In other words, you will be able to narrow down your niche by targeting people who face defined barriers. Let us say, for instance, that you are thinking of teaching a course about working out from home. In talking to your target market, though, you have discovered that their greatest pain points are how expensive workout equipment can be. Now that you know this, you could narrow down your niche and turn it from

"Working Out from Home" to "Working Out from Home Using DIY Equipment."

Another strategy you can adopt to gain better clarity like this is to peruse relevant forums. Platforms like Quora, where copious discussions take place about all kinds of subject matter, can be great for this. The discussions that take place on these forums and the questions that are asked can be very revelatory, in that, they can shed a great deal of light on the problems your audience needs solved. They can give ideas you otherwise might not have considered and thus give you the ability to reach students who might have otherwise passed on your courses.

Once you can identify your audience's problems and pain points, you can write down all your discoveries in your notebook as well. Then you can examine them side by side with your interests, skills, and passions and try to find unique ways to combine them. In doing so you can land on the perfect niche for you. The process of doing so might look a little something like this:

Interest/Skill/Passion	Audience Problem	Niche
SAT Classes	Some students have dyslexia which makes learning complicated TOEFL vocabulary difficult.	SAT Courses for Dyslexic Students
Cooking	Some people are allergic to gluten which narrows down the repertoire of dishes they can make.	Gluten-Free Cooking

Interest/Skill/Passion	Audience Problem	Niche
Web Design	Older adults have trouble understanding certain facets of technology, especially when it comes to web design, but really need to update their websites for business purposes.	Basic Web Design for Older Adults

Conduct Market Research

Of course, your work does not end with just finding your niche. You need to conduct some market research as well. Let's say you have decided to teach "SAT Courses for Dyslexic Students." What does the market look like for such a course? How many students have to take the SAT exam annually in the United States? Seeing as most people who take the SAT are high school students, what percentage of high school students are dyslexic? By considering questions like this, you can figure out how big your target audience is. This means you will be able to see just how many people your courses will appeal to. For this understanding to be accurate, though, you will need to do some market research as well and see who your competition is.

The Competition

Depending on what your specific niche is, you may not have any competition. There might not be a whole lot of people who have thought of teaching "SAT Courses for Dyslexic Students." Then again, you may find out that you actually do have some competition in the market. While that might sound like a bummer, at first, it does not necessarily have to be a bad thing. So long as you do not have too many competitors—so long as your chosen niche is not crowded—you can still succeed in it, if your competitors do one (or all) of three things:

- Provide low-quality content to their students.

- Are not transparent with their students.

- Do not do paid advertising.

If your competition is not providing their students with quality content, then all you will have to do to beat them in your niche will be to provide your prospective students with superior content. You will also have to market your content—that is to say, your courses—really well, which will help you to attract the students you want, but more on that later. Taking a closer look at your competition's content, though, will not just help you to gauge its quality. It'll also enable you to spot what they are lacking in. Let's say you have decided to teach courses on mindful meditation. This is a decidedly saturated niche, meaning there are probably a lot of courses teaching the same subject. However, you noticed that none of your competition offers these courses in Spanish, a language that you happen to be fluent in. You also noticed that very few of the existing courses are about "Using Mindful Meditation to Deal with Post-Traumatic Stress Disorder (PTSD)." The ones that do, offer very low-quality courses and you know that you can do a better job than that. So, you have been able to narrow down your niche in three ways and turn your mindfulness meditation classes into:

- Mindfulness Meditation Courses in Spanish.

- Mindfulness Meditation for Dealing with PTSD.

- Mindfulness Meditation for Dealing with PTSD—in Spanish.

On the other hand, if your competition is transparent, then that means that they are fairly faceless. The students taking their classes do not really connect with the instructor teaching them. This is something that causes audience engagement to be low, even if they are interested in the subject matter being taught. This means that you can easily gain an advantage by creating courses in a personalized way and connecting with your audience.

Finally, you can beat your competition in your niche and make sure you reach more students by using the right marketing strategies—again, more on that later—and perhaps engaging in paid advertising yourself.

Profitability

Your next step is to determine how profitable your niche is. A great way of doing this is to identify trends in the area you have chosen. You can use websites and platforms like Google Trends, Exploding Topics, Answer the Public, and Ubersuggest. Google Trends allows you to search for keywords related to your niche. This allows you to see how popular they are, where they are most used, and what topics are most used with them.

Say that you are going to teach online "Gluten Free Cooking Classes." By doing a search on Google Trends you can see that these keywords are most often searched in Maine, Vermont, New Hampshire, Montana, and Oregon. You can see that the terms are searched about a 100 times per day in the US and that the topics most related to them are "Campfire," "Outdoor Cooking" and "Sourdough Bread." Based on this, you can both determine that your niche will be quite popular and, thus, profitable. You can also come up with topics you can pair it with. For instance, you can decide to make one of the courses you make all about "Gluten Free Campfire Food" or "Gluten Free Sourdough Bread." You can use Answer the Public and Ubersuggest in a similar way, seeing as both are platforms that you use to search for keywords, the same way you do on Google Trends.

Explore Trends

In the meantime, you can use Exploding Topics to find trends that are on the rise. Exploding Topics displays these trends as graphs and shows their upward trajectory over the years. Let us say that you want to teach online courses about "Environmental Governance." If you were to go on Exploding Topics, you'd see that "Environmental, Societal, and Corporate Governance" is a trend that is on the rise. It has, in fact, been on the rise since 2019. This means that the course you want to teach is likely very profitable. If you were to click on "Environmental, Societal and Corporate Governance" and scroll down, you could find related topics that are also on the rise. In that case, you'd see that the topic "Embedded Investment" is a trend as well. You can then use this information to make "Embedded Investment" a part of your "Environmental Governance" courses, thereby making them even more profitable.

Once you have identified trends and looked at how popular the niche you have chosen really is, you can determine its profitability. To accomplish this, you will need to consider a set of different factors:

- **Price**. How should you price your courses, given how common other such courses are in the market, how often your target market searches for it, how your competitors price their courses, and what demand is like?

- **Location**. Where are the learners you are targeting located?

- **Values and Interests**. What do your prospective students value? What are their interests?

- **Demographic**. What kind of student are you targeting as your audience-customer base?

Finally, once you have determined both your niche and how profitable it is, you can and should test it out. To do so, you can create an initial, simple website where the audience you are targeting can find your courses. There, you can offer them free trial courses. Once a student completes a course, you can share a quick survey with them or reach out to them to ask for their feedback and opinions. If your test is not as successful as you wanted it to be, you should not become disheartened. Rather, you should take the feedback that your trial students have given you and use it to improve your courses in any way you can. If, on the other hand, your trial was successful—if students came back to you with glowing reviews and praise—then you can move on to properly launching your courses. That does not mean, of course, that you should not use any feedback you get, regardless of how much your prospective students have praised your courses, to improve them even more.

The Benefits of Finding Your Niche

Finding your niche in the online courses market has a variety of benefits. Some of these benefits are obvious. Others are more on the subtle side. One of these benefits is that identifying your niche can help you to speed up the preparation phase for your courses. In other words, it can help you to plan your course so that it can directly meet the needs and demands of your learners. If you are giving English Speaking Lessons, for instance, you will skip over topics and subjects that you now know your students either do not need or are not all that interested in. Instead, you will be able to focus on the specific topics they need, want, and are interested in. In the process, you will become a greater expert in those areas, and all this will effectively reduce the amount of work you will need to do to plan and prepare for your courses.

A second, more obvious benefit is that your niche will make you stand out among your competitors and the marketplace. When you offer niche online teaching services, you end up attracting students who seek education, tutoring, or direction in specialized areas of study. Seeing that you are designing your courses that can provide them with what they want, rather than create generic courses that seek to please "everyone," makes them more likely to both pick you. It also makes them far more likely to stick with you once they enroll. In time, once you have established a solid following, you can broaden your niches, of course, or adopt more than one, so that you can reach broader and broader pools of audiences.

Another solid benefit is that finding your niche can help you increase your referral rate. A student who leaves your course feeling very satisfied and like they exactly got what they wanted out of it is far more likely to tell a friend about your courses, thinking it might be of interest to them as well. Interestingly enough, this reduces the marketing costs of your online courses. After all, it means that your students are effectively partaking in the marketing process and bringing you more and more customers. All because you understood what they were looking for and delivered it to them. Reducing costs in this way enables you to either save that money you otherwise would have spent or use it in another way to benefit your courses further. You can use it, for instance, to get better quality equipment or software to create your courses with. The improved quality will impact how much your students like your courses and ensure their loyalty even more.

Finding a niche is something that creates the often true impression that you are an expert in your field, which you want to do as an instructor. This infuses your audience with a sense of confidence. It makes them say, "I came to the right address," rather than question your credibility or competence. This, in turn, makes you stand out more in the market and attracts a great number of students your way. Finally, all this obviously increases the profit that you make from your online course, simply by the laws of supply and demand.

Tips for Becoming an Online Course Instructor With Your Very Own Niche

Now that you know how you are supposed to go about identifying your niche and why you really should, the process of doing so might appear to be a little less daunting. Still, it is understandable if the work you need to do feels a little overwhelming. So, here are some tips and tricks of the trade that can help with that:

Try to find overlapping interests, skills, or strengths if you can.

This strategy is usually referred to as finding overlapping competencies. It means identifying different areas that are your strengths and figuring out how you can combine them and turn them into a niche. These areas do not necessarily have to be related to one another, at least not at first glance. Let us say that you want to teach English as a Second Language (ESL) online. This is quite a big and, let us face it, quite a saturated market to tackle. So, how can you narrow it down? Well, what if you realized that one of your strengths is movie analysis? You could combine these two areas to create the niche "ESL Through Movie Analysis?" Wouldn't that be both an engaging and effective way of learning English?

Learn from trial and error.

Just because something sounds like a good idea, does not necessarily mean that it is. This is why the process of finding a niche concludes with a testing phase. The testing phase can show you whether the idea you have landed on will work or not. It can help you understand what you need to do to improve upon your idea to make it work. It can alternatively make you see that an idea simply is not as profitable or functional as you thought it would be. When you see this, though, you can change your idea using what you have learned. Let's say your initial idea was to start "Mindfulness Meditation Courses for Seniors." However, not a lot of seniors were interested in the course. The comments you did receive from those individuals who did participate in your trial courses said something along the lines of, "I wish my 12-year-old nephew could try this." 12-year-olds are a very different audience than seniors of course, but if the comments you receive do indicate that your courses are more suitable for a younger audience and if the subsequent market research you do reveals that this is a niche you could exploit, then why not give it a go?

Ask the right questions when searching for keywords and related topics.

When you are doing keyword and related topic searches to help narrow down your niche or see how profitable it would be, it is important that you ask the right questions. The right questions are those queries that can give you an indication of how popular, in-demand, or sought after a subject is. Examples of such questions would be:

- How many estimated searches have been made for the keyword or topic you have chosen?

- What types of online courses receive the most traffic and attention?

- What online courses out there seem to be the most profitable and popular?

- How popular are these keywords and topics on social media platforms like X?

Conduct a survey among your potential students to better understand what they are looking for and what their pain points are.

Understanding your future customer base's needs is very important if you want to succeed in your niche. A great way of doing this is by having your potential customers take a survey. If you were going to teach an online course called "Coding 101" for instance, you could ask your audience survey questions like:

- What do you struggle most with when it comes to coding?

- What would you most like to see a video or text course in under the coding branch?

- How much would you be willing to spend on such an online course?

- What would you *not* like to see included in an online course about coding?

Find learning gaps.

Finding your niche is actually all about figuring out *who* your audience is. If you do not know who will be taking your courses, after all, how could you tailor your lessons for them? Doing this often requires comprehending who the general market has avoided, ignored, or left out. In other words, it required identifying the learning gaps out there, which you can do by asking yourself the following questions:

- Who in this target group requires additional help and guidance?

- Who would benefit most from my expertise?

- What are their main obstacles in this area?

- What knowledge or skill are they lacking and in need of to progress in this area?

Try to draw on your professional background if you can.

One way to find subjects that you can turn into courses is by looking into your own professional background, even if you are no longer doing a specific job. Let's say you used to be an accountant or venture capitalist in the past and have since retired or changed jobs. Just because you are neither of these things right now, does not mean you can't teach your prospective students about taxes and venture capitalism. Just because you are no longer a veterinarian, does not mean you have forgotten all that you used to know about animal biology. Sure, you may need a refresher on certain things here and there, but you would be getting that anyways when you are preparing for your courses. So, do not hesitate to draw on your professional experience confidently and make use of it in your niche.

Identify your learner's persona.

There is a term called the "buyer's persona" that is often used in the marketing world. The buyer's persona is the profile of the buyer that is going to make use of a product. Within the context of online learning, the "buyer's persona" turns into the "learner's persona". The learner's persona essentially displays all the information you have put together about the learner you are targeting in one single document. It includes things like their obstacles, motivations, age group, gender, and location. Having all this information in one place can help you paint an actual picture of your future learners. It can help you to quickly access their wants, needs, and pain points, without losing any time. This can then, make meeting those wants and needs, and fixing those pain points a much simpler ordeal than it otherwise could have been.

Don't forget "and" when you are searching for keywords online. A good way to gauge if a niche would do well or not is to search for the keywords related to it. You would get even better results, though, if you were to search for certain keywords together. For instance, if your online course is "Understanding Physics Through Yoga," searching for "Yoga" and "Physics" will of course help. Searching for "Yoga" and "Physics," on the other hand, might help more. So might search for "Yoga" + "Physics" and "Yoga," "Physics."

Know the popular niches to exploit.

As you work on determining what your specific niche is, do some research about what popular, larger niches are in the current online courses market. While these figures are bound to change in the coming years, the most popular online course types of 2022, were:

- **Fitness Courses.** Though this niche has always been popular it has experienced significant growth in recent years. In 2015, for instance, the market for it was worth $542 billion. By 2017, that figure had grown to $595.4 billion, meaning that it has an annual growth rate of 4.8%.

- **Parenting Courses.** It is understandable why this would be a popular course, especially considering the homeschooling situation many parents found themselves in 2020. From child development to teaching kids at home and to first aid for newborns, this niche has a lot of room for exploration.

- **DIY and Decoration Courses.** This is another niche that gained popularity with the work from home and lockdown situation of the pandemic. According to one survey, 77% of all DIY projects that people undertake are for interior decoration purposes and 47% of all homeowners engage in these projects. This makes DIY and Decoration courses a clearly lucrative niche to dive into.

- **Creative Writing Courses.** It seems everyone decided to try their hand at being a writer when the pandemic hit, and the trend does not seem to be going away any time soon. After all, the creative writing industry is expected to undergo an 8% growth between 2016 and 2026. So, why not jump into the fray and be a part of the movement, either by showing people how to pound out a novel or even a good book proposal?

- **Anti-Aging and Beauty Courses.** Online makeup tutorials have always been rather popular, so it should not be all that surprising to find out that the beauty niche could be a good option to explore for your online course. The fact that the beauty industry has only been growing since 2017 adds to that fact. The industry has reached a market size of $1082.9 billion in that year alone, meaning that it has an average growth rate of 4.1%. So, jumping on this bandwagon would not just be understandable, it would also be incredibly practical.

- **Online Marketing Courses**. Online marketing has become an essential part of any business and industry. It is something even you will have to take advantage of when you are marking your own course. That means that you will have no shortage of learners if you were to try and teach courses on this matter. Most of these customers would like to be in the process of or want to start their own small business, so that might be one way to narrow down your niche. Others might be to focus on content marketing and content creation, social media marketing, and affiliate marketing.

- **Coding Classes**. Coding is another booming area that everyone wants to take advantage of. It is an incredibly valued skill and job prospects for people who know how to code are expected to be nothing short of incredible in the coming years. This plainly means you have a lot of potential students who are eager to learn, if only to keep climbing up the professional ladder in their careers.

- **Foreign Language Courses**. Knowing another language is something that can increase the salary that an individual makes by about 15%. It is also something that increases people's job prospects, especially in the ever more global world that we live in. Therefore, it too is a niche that you could consider exploiting, if you have any foreign languages tucked in your back pocket.

- **Art Courses**. Like creative writing courses, art courses have been drawing more and more interest over the years. This is partly because it is a good creative outlet which many people turn to as a hobby or stress relief. Hence, art therapy is a thing, for instance. Since basic art courses, like drawing, do not require a lot of materials to get started, and certainly not expensive ones, they make for a good niche.

- **Cooking Courses**. This is another area that has been drawing more and more interest over the years. Lots of people took to cooking for the first time during the pandemic. Lots more decided to expand on their skills and that is to say nothing of those individuals whose dietary requirements changed—perhaps they became vegan, started the ketogenic diet, or discovered they have a gluten allergy. This means that there are a lot of ways cooking courses can be managed and that many different niches can be born from it.

Finding your niche can be a bit of a process as you have seen, but you will undoubtedly be able to find the right one for you by putting some work and thought into it. Coming up with your niche, though, is obviously just the first step to launching your online courses. There are many more steps to come, starting with creating a syllabus and preparing your course materials.

Checklist

	Determine what your interests and expertise are
	Identify your students and their needs, and create a student persona
	Find unique ways to combine your skills to solve your prospective students' problems
	Conduct market research and identify your competition
	Identify your value proposition
	Determine how profitable your niche is
	Explore trends to see what is popular
	Do keyword and topic research and find learning gaps
	Draw on your personal educational and professional background

Chapter 2:
Creating a Syllabus and Course Materials

So, you have decided to start an online course. You've thought long and hard about the niche you want, completed your research, and concretely defined your course. The next things to do are to create a syllabus and prepare your course materials, in that order. A syllabus is essentially a document, filled with important information about your class, such as what subjects you will be covering and what assignments will be due, and when. Course materials, on the other hand, are the materials you will use to actually teach your course. These can include any videos you make, assignments you prepare, quizzes you give, and more. You will need to prepare both of these things before you can even think about launching your online course.

How to Create a Good Syllabus

Your syllabus is something that works in concert with your curriculum. Your curriculum is the subjects you will be teaching throughout the course of your, well, course. The two essentially lay out how you are going to teach the subjects you have decided on, what resources you will use to teach them and how the individual lessons supporting and communicating those subjects will be structured.

You need to have a good syllabus at hand for several reasons. The first is that it can keep you from becoming overwhelmed. This is doubly true for those who are new to online teaching, though veteran instructors need syllabi as well. This is because your syllabus clearly maps out everything that you have to do for each and every class. This enables you to both confidently navigate your courses and to prepare for them properly. It reduces any confusion or hesitation you may experience when teaching and puts you at the top of your game.

A syllabus is not just important for online course instructors. It is equally as important for learners and students partaking in those courses as well. Providing students with syllabi means clearly communicating what your expectations of them are. It also means preparing them for courses to come, seeing as it'll inform them about when assignments are due and what they will learn in the days and weeks to come. A syllabus then proves useful for both you, as an instructor, and any learners that will be taking your course.

Creating a good syllabus begins with the simple act of writing down your course name. You think of your course name as your syllabus title. The course name, like any good title, must clearly and concisely communicate what the learners and students will be learning. In other words, it should neither be something overly long nor anything complicated. Short and sweet will do. After you have written down your course name, you move on to describing basic course and instructor information. This will mean providing the following info:

- Instructor name.

- Instructor contact information.

- Duration of the course.

- How long individual lessons will take.

- Prerequisites of the course for instance whether a learner needs to have taken another course before taking the one whose syllabus you are writing.

- The format of the course, which will be online, in this case.

- A brief course description.

- List of required texts and materials.

- List of recommended texts and materials.

- List of materials the learner needs to succeed in the course.

Course Description

Of the items that make up the "Basic Course Information" section of the syllabus, it is the course description you will have to devote most of your time and attention to. The brief course description is a paragraph giving an overview of your course, including what content it will be covering, which skills and knowledge it will teach, and how it will benefit the learner overall. The key thing about the course description is that it should be concise and as clear as possible.

You should make sure that your course description is no longer than 125 words. It would be best if the sentences making up the course description began with verbs as often as possible. They should always be written with student-centric focus and in both the present tense and using the active voice. It should also avoid doing certain kinds of things, such as:

- Beginning with the words "this course."

- Using deliverables like "participants will learn" and use wording like "participants will gain the opportunity to learn" instead.

- Including the names of any text, software, technology, or other kinds of material that will likely have changed the following year in the description.

Resources

Once you have completed the course description, you will be able to work on the "Required Text" section. Here you will need to provide all textbooks, books, and other written materials that learners will need, in order to complete the course. For simplicity's sake, let us say that you intend to include Yuval Noah Harari's *Sapiens: A Brief History of Humankind* in this section. To properly list this work, you will need to write its full name, the full name of its author, its ISBN, the edition, and provide information as to where it can be found and in what format. You can also give a short description of the book, if you would like. The same rules will apply to your "Recommended Reading

Section." You will of course, need to specify where and how your learners and students can find or access each item touched on in this part of the syllabus.

While you are at it, you should write down all course requirements as well. This can include any and all texts that need to be read as part of the course, any tests and quizzes that need to be passed and how they'll be graded, any projects and assignments that need to be completed, and how students can both access and submit them and finally, what guidelines students need to follow when completing those assignments.

Course Goals and Objectives

Next up in your syllabus will be the course goals. The course goals are what learners will strive to achieve by taking your course. It should be noted though, that a course goal is not the same thing as a learning objective. A course goal refers to the overall aim of a course. A learning objective, on the other hand, is one of the steps that a learner will have to take on the way to achieving their course goal. Typically, lesson objectives are the goals of individual classes. For instance, "learning trigonometric functions" could be the learning objective of a single lesson given as part of a trig course. In the same vein, "learning the crane pose" might be the lesson objective of a particular session or day.

To write a good course objective, you need to start your sentence with an action verb. This verb has to be related to the action that you want your learners to complete by taking your course. A good course should also explain the knowledge, skill, or practice that the learner should have learned. A couple of examples of such a course goal would be:

- If you have learned U.S. immigration history, you will be able to explain how immigration has impacted the cultural makeup of the United States.

- If you have learned the blanching technique, you will be able to blanch cauliflower heads without issues.

- If you have learned how to do fractional stitches, you will be able to do ½ and ¼ stitches without any problems.

As you may have noticed, I have used the word "action verbs" both when talking about course descriptions and course goals. These are verbs that can adequately express the actions that individuals are either doing or have done. Strong action verbs that you can use in your syllabus, course description, and course goals fall into one of six categories: those related to remembering, those related to understanding, those that mean applying a concept or technique, those that have to do with analyzing, those that refer to evaluating and those that have to do with creating. Some examples of action verbs that fall into these categories and that you can freely use are:

Remember	Understand	Analyze	Evaluate	Apply	Create
Recall	Express	Classify	Conclude	Prepare	Hypothesize
List	Demonstrate	Breakdown	Judge	Organize	Produce
Outline	Illustrate	Identify	Asses	Use	Design
Draw	Summarize	Differentiate	Measure	Graph	Formulate

Course Calendar

Now, the more complicated part of preparing a syllabus begins with creating a course calendar. Your course calendar is the go-to reference your learners will use to keep track of upcoming courses and assignments and review what will be covered in that particular class.

This calendar must contain the following information:

- Time the course starts.

- Time the course ends.

- How long each course lasts.

- When assignments are due.

- Any other dates of interest.

Each course that is positioned in the calendar should include a brief description of what will be explored in that course, what the learner will be able to do after learning it, what the assignments related to it are, and when those assignments need to be completed. You can also list the learning objectives of each course, along with the activities that will be done as part of the course. The learning objectives you list should, of course, be measurable and have clear, definable outcomes. These outcomes are what are known as learning outcomes. Learning outcomes are what you need to use to shape your course schedule. This means that you need to start the process of creating your course calendar or schedule by defining the objective of each and every course.

Let us say the online course you are teaching is made up of 12 sessions in total, spread over four weeks. This means you will be holding three sessions per week. For argument's sake, let us say that you chose to air these sessions every Monday, Wednesday, and Friday at 7 p.m., though of course, you can choose any other day and time as suits your personal schedule. Once you have settled on this, you will have to sit down and define your course goal. After defining your course goal, you will have to ask yourself the question, "What 12 learning objectives (steps) can help my learners to achieve this goal?" In answering this question, you will write down 12 separate learning objectives; one for each session or lesson. Next, you will have to consider which teaching approaches and assignments will best help your learners and students internalize what you want them to learn. Will a video lecture be best for communicating your message and helping you to achieve this? Will having your learners make a presentation about what they are learning to be better?

You will be able to figure out how you want to conduct each and every one of these classes by asking yourself these questions. Before you know it, you will have basic class structures in your hand, which you can work to refine and strengthen.

To make all this information a little more concrete, let us take a look at what a sample course syllabus would look like for a 12-course program:

COURSE NAME

Instructor Name:

Contact Information:

Best Times to Contact:

Expected Instructor Response Times:

Course Description:

_____

_____

_____

Required Course Materials:

_____

_____

_____

Suggested Course Materials:

_____

_____

_____

Required Technology for Course:

Learner Requirements and Expectations:

Course Goals:

_____

Course Schedule:

- **Course 1:** Subject

  - Learning Objectives, Approach, Assignments and Assignment Due Dates

- **Course 2:** Subject

  - Learning Objectives, Approach, Assignments and Assignment Due Dates

- **Course 3:** Subject

  - Learning Objectives, Approach, Assignments and Assignment Due Dates

- **Course 4:** Subject

  - Learning Objectives, Approach, Assignments and Assignment Due Dates

- **Course 5:** Subject

  - Learning Objectives, Approach, Assignments and Assignment Due Dates

- **Course 6:** Subject

  - Learning Objectives, Approach, Assignments and Assignment Due Dates

- **Course 7:** Subject

- Learning Objectives, Approach, Assignments and Assignment Due Dates

- **Course 8:** Subject

  - Learning Objectives, Approach, Assignments and Assignment Due Dates

- **Course 9:** Subject

  - Learning Objectives, Approach, Assignments and Assignment Due Dates

- **Course 10:** Subject

  - Learning Objectives, Approach, Assignments and Assignment Due Dates

- **Course 11:** Subject

  - Learning Objectives, Approach, Assignments and Assignment Due Dates

- **Course 12:** Subject

  - Learning Objectives, Approach, Assignments and Assignment Due Dates

Grading System and Policy (if applicable):

Late Work Policy:

Viewing Grades (if applicable):

Course Policies: A description of how students are expected to behave through the online course.

Incomplete Policy:

Keys to Planning an Effective Online Class

There are several keys to creating a well-organized, understandable, and effective online class. One of these is to create solid lesson plans. Your lesson plan is a thorough plan laying out how you will go about conducting a specific lesson or session. Basically, it is a more detailed version of the learning objectives, approach, assignments, and assignment due dates that you list in your syllabus. Making lesson plans is a very important part of online teaching and tutoring. This is because it grants you a greater sense of clarity and allows you to go into each course confidently.

Making a good lesson plan starts with focusing on your lesson objectives, which you have already defined when working on your syllabus. But let us take a closer look at these objectives now. How exactly are you supposed to determine a lesson objective anyway? How can you make sure that the lesson objective you wrote is a good one? The answer is simple: by following SMART goals.

SMART goals are a technique people use when they are setting goals for themselves, be they personal, academic, work and business related or something else entirely. The very term SMART is actually an acronym that stands for:

- specific

- measurable

- attainable

- relevant

- time based

If you are following SMART goal rules when setting your lesson objectives, then, you have to make sure that they meet these criteria. This means that your learning objectives have to be specific, rather than vague, easy to measure and thus track, attainable by all the learners that take your courses, relevant to your students and your class, and time-based, in that they can be achieved in the time frame that your syllabus lays out.

If you are going over your lesson objectives, and they are too vague or hard to accomplish in the time that you have allotted them, then you may want to revise them. Once you are satisfied with your lesson objectives, you can ask yourself which materials you will use to achieve them and what your lesson procedure will look like. The materials you use can be anything from videos to texts and visuals. As for your lesson procedure, that is the step-by-step process you will use to walk your learners through the subject you are teaching them that day.

Of course, to write down your lesson procedure for a particular day, you will first have to determine which activities you will use to meet your lesson objectives. In determining this, you can ask yourself the following questions:

- How will you start introducing your learners to the subject at hand?

- What is the best way for you to communicate this information to them?

- What activities can you make part of the learning process so that the learners use their critical thinking and problem-solving skills?

- Are there any real-life situations and scenarios you can use as examples when discussing this subject? If so, what are they?

- What kinds of group or solo activities can your learners do to put the information they've obtained into practice?

Applied Educational Structure (AES)

You can begin creating a rough outline of your lesson plan for a particular day by answering these questions. You can then detail and solidify it further by deciding on a teaching strategy. Most online instructors use a strategy known as Applied Educational Structure (AES), though plenty of in-person instructors utilize this methodology as well. The AES strategy is made up of four phases which you can apply to your lesson plan.

These phases are:

- exploration

- learning and practice

- reflection

- reinforcement

The exploration phase of AES is where you explore the subject that you are sharing with your learners. It is where you introduce its key concepts and your lesson objective. Usually, this phase adopts a lecture format, which works particularly well with online courses, as you might have guessed.

The learning and practice phase, on the other hand, is the portion of the course where you have your students work independently or together to better understand the concepts they've learned and put them into practice. If, for instance, you have included a text that further explains something, this phase would be when your students read it. If you have guided notes in your course materials, this is also when your students would make use of them. This phase could also include various group or class activities that you deem necessary.

The reflection phase is where your students reflect on what they have learned. They can do this through course discussion—either live, if you are using something like Zoom, or on your course's message board. This is when students turn to their critical thinking and problem-solving skills. This means that this is also when you would pose interesting questions for your students to try and answer or problems they'd strive to solve. Said questions and problems would, of course, be related to what they had just learned. A Q&A session might also take place in this phase, if your online course model is live and thus allows for it.

The final phase of AES is reinforcement, where, as per the name, your students reinforce what they have learned. They could do this both in group activities and individually. This is what in-class tasks and assignments with due dates are for.

There are two other steps that are part of the AES process, though they are not considered to be among its phases. These are the assessment and lesson reflection. The assessment is the part of the course where you gauge how well your students have learned what you have been teaching them and whether they've been able to meet the lesson objectives. There are a myriad of techniques you can use to assess your students' progress, such as, but not limited to giving them pop quizzes or quizzes, having them write essays, making them keep class journals, and making them do class presentations or even group presentations.

As for the lesson reflection, this is the part of the course where you give yourself honest feedback about what you could have done differently and what you can improve upon. Such feedback is invaluable for online courses, at least if you want them to have longevity. Giving yourself honest feedback requires asking yourself the right questions. Some examples of questions you can ask yourself during this step are:

- Was there a portion of the course where students required more help?

- Did any particular subject or topic take a longer time to get through than anticipated?

- Is there any part of the course that the students breezed through?

- Were all the lesson objectives met by most, if not all the students?

- Was the course goal met by most, if not all the students?

- Were the students engaged and interested in every lesson or did their attention wane sometimes? If the latter, when, specifically, did their attention and interest wane?

Answering these questions honestly and looking at how a course went objectively can give you invaluable insights. You can then use these insights to revise your course as needed and even come up with different iterations of it.

Creating solid lesson plans, though, is just one key to planning an effective online class. Another is understanding your students, which you should have made some headway on when you were working on identifying your niche. Understanding your students is important because when you do, you become able to create a lesson plan, course schedule, and syllabus that actually meets their needs. Taking some extra time to really connect with your students and grasp where they are coming from can significantly improve the quality of your course.

Another key to planning an effective online class is to keep teaching modules, that is to say the methods you use to teach them, such as video lectures, relatively short. If you keep your online teaching modules long, then you run the risk of losing your students' interest and attention. Human beings' average attention spans are quite short, after all. For reference, the attention span of an average teen—say someone around 14 years of age—is between 28 to 42 minutes. Meanwhile the average attention span of audiences is eight to 10 minutes. This being the case, keeping your online lectures and other teaching methodologies short and interesting is to your benefit. But how exactly can you go about doing that?

Planning Lectures and Deciding How to Structure Your Course

If you want your students to be engaged in the courses that you teach and actually learn what you are sharing with them, then you have to keep your lectures short, clear, and interesting. One way you can accomplish this is to use plenty of visual elements in your lesson. This works particularly well when you are giving a presentation, for instance. The good thing about visuals is that they have the power and ability to communicate lengthy information with just a few quick tidbits. You know, a picture is worth a thousand words, and all that. Graphs and charts, for instance, can do this really well. So can humorous illustrations and colorful photos.

Another way of keeping your lectures short but engaging is to segment them into bite-sized chunks, of say eight to 10 minutes, considering how long an audience's attention span is. Let's say that you recorded a video tutorial about a DIY shelf or story writing for beginners. Let's also say that the tutorial is 40 minutes long. You can go over the video and segment it into four eight-to-10-minute-long parts. You can then upload these parts onto your platform, thereby allowing your students to go through them at their own pace. A student, for instance, would be able to watch them all together, if they wanted to. They could also watch two in the morning and two in the afternoon or one every day until they watched them all. This freedom that you would afford them would allow them to work their lessons into busy schedules and get to them in their own time, so long as they completed classes and assignments on time, of course.

You can also consider utilizing a technique known as flipping the classroom. Flipping the classroom is a learning method where you have your students in-class activities, like listening to podcasts or watching short videos, for instance, before the class, instead of during. The students thus come to the online class prepared and you spend your time doing assignments and activities with them, rather than lecturing. In other words, you "flip" the order of the class. Flipping the classroom is a great method to adopt for online courses and lectures because it has actually been proven to increase student retention—meaning how much they remember from class—and engagement—meaning how involved they are in class. But that is not the only benefit that this method affords. There are, in fact, many others. For instance, a flipped classroom can:

- Create a more interactive learning environment.

- Make students take more active roles in their learning experience, rather than a passive one.

- Increase communication between students and instructor.

- Give the learners and students more of an opportunity to learn at their own pace.

- Increase students focus and attention in class.

- Allow for deep learning and greater reflection.

- Make instructors get to know and understand their students better.

- Provide instructors with videos that they can use repeatedly for the same classes over the years.

If you want to adopt the flipped classroom methodology for your lectures and online courses, then your first step will have to be clearly explaining what you want your students to do and achieve. In other words, you will have to explain what video they need to watch or materials they need to read before class and how you will be doing activities about them in class. That done, you will obviously have to choose which materials you want your students to spend time with before class. These materials can be presentations, online video tutorials, online reading materials, or podcasts. Once you have shared these materials with your students, you should communicate how they are supposed to ask any questions they may have about what they've learned. For instance, you can tell them to email you any questions they have about the subjects they've read or watched videos about. You can also direct them to a message board on your course page, where they can post their questions. It goes without saying that if and when a student reaches out to you with a question after going through the materials, you need to get back to them with an answer in a reasonable time frame.

Naturally, you need a way to ascertain whether or not your students have done the work and learned what they were supposed to. There are several activities you can do to achieve this. Such activities can take the form of quizzes, online or live discussion forums, and Q&A sessions. It can also take the form of concept maps. A concept map is a visual representation of the different elements making up a concept that a student has learned and tracing how they are connected to one another. Seeing as this can be very illustrative of what a student has learned, you can ask your students to create concept maps in class. Alternatively, you can have them write summaries of what they have learned and share them with you and maybe even with their peers.

On the day of a lesson, you will be focusing on activities that are designed to put what your students have learned into practice. These can be both individual activities and group activities. If you are going with individual activities, you can have your students take multiple-choice polls, create more concept maps, as well as mind maps, and give oral presentations. If you are going with group activities, you can have your students partake in class discussions, start debates, just to name a few.

Preparing the Right Course Materials and Assignments

You can plan the best lectures and courses in the world, but they will not mean as much if they are not paired with the right course materials and assignments. But what do we mean when we say the "right" course material and assignments? Course materials refer to the written, visual, and aural materials you use to teach your course. The assignments refer to the work you assign your students so that they can practice and internalize what they have learned.

As mentioned before, the right course materials are ones that are relatively short and use plenty of visuals, as this will help you to keep your students engaged. It will also lower the risk of their attention wandering off. To choose the best possible materials for your course, you need to start the selection process well in advance. You can find the ones you want to use among materials you have from any previous courses you may have taught, passages selected from texts, video clips you find on YouTube, and more. Better yet you can create presentations that are filled with helpful visuals, charts, graphs, and the like, rather than lines upon lines of text snaking after one another.

Just because your course content should have plenty of visuals, does not mean they should not provide explanations and rationales as to why something is a certain way. If you are teaching an online course about founding LLCs, for instance, and mention that the owner of a single–member LLC is required to pay self–employment tax, you should not just leave it at that. You should go on to explain why that is the case, using the course materials you have found or created.

The key thing to watch when it comes to course materials is making sure that they align with the learning objectives of the lessons they are a part of. If you can, take a look at the course content that your competition provides their students with and try to fill in the gaps they have left in their education plans. Try to integrate questions into your course materials—such as presentations, for instance—that you can ask your students mid-class. This can make a massive difference in how well your students retain the information that they are given. If you have had your students read a passage from a text, for example, you can ask them a couple of questions about it. Once they are done, you can share what the correct answers are and begin a class discussion about them.

What about the right assignments then? How do you choose or create them? You start by reviewing your course goal and lesson objectives along with your students' levels. The assignments you give to someone who's new to astrophysics or herb gardening will not be the same as someone who has taken several courses in these areas before. This holds true when you are choosing and preparing your course materials as well, but I digress. When you are evaluating your lesson objectives in an effort to come up with assignments for your students, you should ask yourself the following questions:

- What do you want the project or assignment you will be giving to establish or reinforce?

- What information, skills, abilities, or knowledge do you want this project or assignment to measure?

- What are the most difficult aspects of your course for your students? In other words, what needs to be reinforced more?

- What difference do you want to make in your students' lives?

For example, let's say that you want the assignment you are giving to your students to measure their critical thinking skills. If that is the case, having them analyze a passage that you assign them, rather than simply reading or summarizing it might be a good idea.

Once you understand what exactly, you want to achieve by giving a specific assignment, you will be able to tailor that assignment accordingly. To accentuate this effect, though, you should follow certain rules while structuring your assignments:

- **Provide your students with a detailed explanation of the assignment in question**. This actually makes students more successful when completing their assignments. Given that, you should not stop at defining assignments in your course syllabus.

You should provide your students with assignment handouts as well. These handouts should make all the steps necessary for completing that assignment clearly. As an added benefit, this practice can help students to manage their time better and keep from spending unnecessary lengths trying to figure out what exactly they should do.

- **Use open-ended questions in assignments**. Open-ended questions are better than closed, "yes or no" questions in that they really get students thinking. This allows them to really internalize what they are learning, rather than simply memorize it.

- **Give students the opportunity to make their assignments their own**. This means giving students the opportunity to personalize their assignments, which increases both their engagement and retention levels. As such, having a student prepare their very own presentation on something will be much more effective in helping them to really learn than having them answer a bunch of questions about it.

- **Don't give assignments that are too long**. A lot of instructors often give assignments that are too long in a well-meaning effort to provide them with a challenge. This usually backfires though, as it causes students to lose focus. If you have an assignment that seems too long, one way to shorten it might be to divide it into sequential portions. This will allow your students to tackle the assignment in smaller bits rather than as one long, continuous thing. This will, in turn, make it easier for them to retain their focus and do well on their assignment.

- **Don't suggest that there is a perfect or ideal response that your students can give in the assignment.** Contrary to what you might think, making such a suggestion will not push your students to try their best. Instead, it will limit their thinking, sometimes making them blind to the most obvious answer. It can also cause the students to doubt themselves and the answers they've given. As a result, they might keep changing their answer and give a wrong one, when the one they had originally gone with was correct.

- **Be as specific as you can be in the assignment directions and guidelines**. Asking your students to discuss a concept after they've just learned it is, unfortunately, a bit vague. Asking them whether a particular experiment would work, given the concept they just learned, however, is not. This is because the latter is the kind of question with a very specific direction and answer, as well as one that gets students to actively use their critical thinking skills.

So, you have created your syllabus, devised your lesson plans, prepared your lectures and how they are going to go, and even determined both your course materials and the assignments you are going to be giving. You are now ready to start your course, right? Not quite because this is not an in-person course, as you will remember. Rather, it is an online one, which means you have to put everything you have prepared, well, online. More specifically, you have to use certain kinds of software, programs, and technologies to make your course available to your prospective students. We will cover this in the next chapter.

Checklist

	Write a course description (no longer than 125 words)
	Determine what textbooks and other resources students will require
	Set out course goals and objectives
	Create a course calendar
	Set SMART goals
	Plan lectures and lay out lesson structures
	Prepare course materials and assignments

Chapter 3:
How to Use Different Platforms for Online Courses

Online courses may have been a novelty once upon a time, but today, that is no longer the case. The market for online courses was steadily growing before 2020, but when the pandemic arrived, it experienced a truly terrifying boom. Suddenly, all these platforms were opening up, which people could use to start all sorts of courses, exploring every manner of subject. At the same time, all these institutions of higher learning, meaning universities and colleges, were offering online courses that students could enroll in. In fact, according to one survey more than 30% of such institutions are currently offering online courses. The COVID–19 pandemic and the following lockdowns obviously played a huge role in this. However, the situation neither changed nor went away with the pandemic. Instead, the online courses market only kept growing and likely will continue to do so. Arguably, online courses will change what education will look like going forward, if it hasn't begun to do so already. So, why precisely is this the case? Why are online courses so popular, both among instructors and students, and why should you consider starting one in the first place?

Why Should I Start an Online Course?

There are many, many reasons for an instructor, such as yourself, to start an online course. The first is the obvious financial incentive it gives instructors and potential instructors. You see, an online course is neither too difficult nor too costly to start. If anything, it is simple and affordable, something anyone can do. Conversely, though, it is something that can become a steady source of income for an instructor, without requiring that they constantly create new content. So long as the original content that they create—meaning their course—is of good quality and so long as they market it well, they will have to do very little work to keep it generating an income. At most, they may have to update here and there, every once in a while, just to make sure that it remains abreast of the latest developments related to the field it is teaching. But beyond that? An online instructor will have to put in little to no work once they have created their course and started the marketing process.

Income

Don't believe me? Currently, the online courses market is worth a grand total of $300 billion. An instructor can make anything from $1,000 to $100,000 per year from their online courses. How much they make will typically depend on how many students they manage to bring into their courses, what their conversation rate—the rate at which they are able to convert people who click on their ads to customers using their course—and what the price of their courses are. As an example, if you had 10,000 potential students click on your online course, and if your conversion rate was 2%, if the price of a single course was $89, you would end up making $17,800.

While that is not a bad sum to make, a 2% conversion rate is considered to be low. The average conversion rate for online classes, at present, is 3–5%. What you ideally want is to have a conversion rate of 6–10% or over 11%, if you can. How you will be able to do that, though, will be covered in the marketing section of this book. So, for now, let us turn our attention to some of the other benefits that online courses offer instructors, starting with flexibility.

Flexibility

Unlike traditional, in-person courses, online courses allow instructors to be very flexible with their time. This makes it easy for them to manage their time well and do quality work without having to rush. For one thing, starting an online course means not having to waste time stuck in traffic or commuting in any other way. For another, it means being able to hold lessons when it suits their schedule, assuming they are doing "live" lessons. However, online courses do not have to be live. They can be pre-recorded and released on a schedule. This means that instructors can record and prepare their courses in advance and just post them on a pre-arranged date and time. The time that instructors save in this way is immensely valuable. That is time they can devote to other things, after all, including helping students who need more guidance, evaluating course work and even just relaxing a little and spending more time with their family and loved ones. This latter can prevent burnout among instructors. According to a poll taken in 2022, one out of every 10 K–12 teachers said that they felt burned out at some point or another. The downtime that online teaching affords instructors, though, works wonders in preventing this. That being the case, the fact that many teachers, including university professors, prefer giving online courses to their students is not all that surprising.

This burnout-preventative effect is compounded by the very simple fact that online courses allow instructors to work from the comfort of their homes, as well as from anywhere in the world, so long as they have a stable internet connection. An online instructor can just as easily set up a workstation in a corner of their home, just as they can set up a workout zone, with a Pilates mat and dumbbells, if they are teaching a more physical course, like "Strength Training for Seniors." An added benefit of this is that instructors are able to decorate and organize their "work zone" however they'd like. It can be as organized or cluttered, colorful or simplistic as they would like it to be. The kind of environment that an individual works in can have a great effect on their overall mood and productivity, as you may know. Studies show that people tend to be more productive when they get to work in environments they actually like, after all. This work-from-home situation, then, can be both very comfortable for instructors and make them more productive than they otherwise might have been. Of course, for that to truly be the case, instructors need to keep their work zone clearly separated from their living spaces.

Reduced Administrative Work

Another unique way in which online courses help instructors save time is by reducing the amount of administrative work that they have to do. Sadly, traditional teachers spend more time doing administrative work than they do teaching their students. This simply is not the case for teachers and instructors who teach online courses. The administrative work that teachers typically have to do includes planning lessons, marking assignments, quizzes, and tests, drafting proposals, accounting for spending, taking daily attendance, and more. When teachers and instructors switch to online teaching, though, they often find that they do not have to do so many things like these, because the system they are using takes care of them. For instance, most online teaching software automatically takes students' attendance, without the instructor having to bother to do so. This might seem like a small thing, but such small things add up. When you think of it like that, it is easy to understand how online courses can save teachers hours at a time by taking care of tasks that would take minutes in and of themselves.

Online teaching also makes it very easy for teachers to update their course materials and content. This is one of the main reasons why a course you create now can be used again 10, 15, or even 20 years from now, so long as you make a couple of tweaks. The platforms you will have used to create and launch your online course usually make such tweaks and adjustments very easy to do.

Interestingly enough, online teaching actually is a lot more sustainable, in the environmental sense, than in-person teaching. So, if you are someone who cares about things like global warming and recycling, this should be an appealing benefit for you. Online teaching is able to accomplish this because, unlike traditional teaching, it does not require that you hand out a bunch of worksheets and presentations as printed-out handouts to your students. Instead, you can deliver them to your students as PDFs, Word documents, and other digital formats. Your students can then take a look at those documents on their computers, smartphones, or other electronic devices.

Benefits for Learners and Students

Of course, online courses do not just have benefits for instructors and teachers. They offer numerous advantages to the learners and students taking them as well. Much like instructors, online learning allows students to cut back on things like commute times. It also allows them to work from the comfort of their own homes or, again, anywhere around the world. This means that a student in India can take a college course being offered in the United States, without having to move an inch from their living room. What's more, they can do this without having to spend a lot of money, the way they would have had to do if they were to fly to the United States, organize visas, accommodation, pay tuition to the college in question and attend the class in person.

Another great advantage of online courses is that the software and programs they use make learning easier for students by accommodating their learning styles. Such programs and software use various algorithms to identify students' learning patterns and use what they discover to personalize the content to fit those patterns. If a student is particularly struggling with a concept, the algorithm in question can adjust the way that concept is explained or presented to them. This understandably improves the speed at which individuals are able to learn. At the same time, it gives shy and more reticent students greater opportunities to participate in class discussions by moving said discussions onto things like message boards.

Finally, online courses allow students to learn at their own pace, rather than constantly having to rush to catch up. This reduces the pressure that students are under significantly, as well as the resultant stress they would typically experience. This makes it easier for non-traditional students, such as older adults who did not get to pursue the education they wanted when they were younger, for instance, to pursue the degrees or classes they want. It even levels out the playing field for disabled students, who might not have been able to go after the degrees they wanted because the institutions that offered them did not accommodate for their needs. If a student is deaf, for instance, learning on a college campus might be very difficult, unless the instructor knows sign language. Let us face it, more often than not, they do not. If, on the other hand, they were to sign up for an online course, they would not face the same challenge, because they could just turn on the closed captioning—that is to say subtitles—feature of the learning platform they were using.

Platforms for Online Courses

Now that you know the many advantages that online courses offer to instructors and students alike, the question you must be asking yourself is, "How do I create one for myself?" In truth, there are several different kinds of platforms that you can use. These platforms are Teachable, Podia, Thinkific, Kajabi, LearnDash, and Udemy, respectively. All of them work in different ways, for the most part, though their key features tend to be similar. So, how do you choose which platform is the right one for you? To make this choice, you will first have to understand how they work, how you can create user accounts on them, how you navigate them, and what their advantages and disadvantages are. With that in mind, let us take a closer look at the online teaching platforms at your fingertips, starting with…

Teachable

Teachable is an online teaching and learning platform that was founded in 2013, by an entrepreneur named Ankur Nagpal. At the time the platform was known as Fedora. In 2015, however, it became Teachable as we know it. In 2020, Teachable officially had more than 100,000 instructors teaching courses on the platform. As of January 2023, they had over 37 million e-learners using the platform, offered more than 417,000 courses, and had more than 123,000 instructors on board.

The first step to using Teachable as an instructor is to set up your own account or "school". Your "school" is your primary Teachable website. This is where your courses will be hosted. To create this website, you first have to go on Teachable and click on "Create a School." There, you enter your first name and last name, then create a password, before clicking on the "I agree to the Terms of Use and Privacy Policy" button. All that done, you click on the "Create Account" button. Next, you will be taken to the page called "Create Your School," where you need to choose a name for your school, which you are allowed to change later, if you'd like. For argument's sake, let us say you have decided to name your school "Black Ink Writing School." You enter that into the space you are given and click on, "Create Your School."

Once you do that, you are taken to an optional survey. Regardless of whether or not you complete the survey, your next step is to click on the button "Enter My School."

Once you enter your school, you will be able to create your first course. Courses are referred to as "products" on Teachable. You can find the option to create your product on the dashboard that appears when you enter your school. Your dashboard includes a menu on the left side of the page, with the following items:

Dashboard

- Users

- Site

- Sales

- Emails

- Settings

Products +

- Courses

- Coaching

- Bundles

You see that "+" next to "Products?" You have to click on that in order to create your first course. When you click on it, you are automatically given the option to choose between creating a course and a coaching program. If you go with a course, you will be choosing to create contents and assignments, which your students will access and use later. If you go with a coaching program, you will essentially be choosing to have live, pre-scheduled video chat sessions with people.

For simplicity's sake, let us say that you have selected "create a course." You are now taken to a page where you can choose the name of your course. Let us say that you have decided to name it "Short Story Writing 101." You enter that under "Course Title" and then enter your name beneath "Author." Next, you click on "Continue" which will take you to the Curriculum tab. This is the page you use to upload your content, that is to say, your video tutorials, presentations, and the like. The first thing you should upload to your course is your syllabus. To achieve this, you first have to get to the files and documents waiting in your computer and rename them as "Section 1 – Lecture 1," "Section 1 – Lecture 2," "Section 2 – Lecture 1," and so forth. This is because courses are divided into sections on Teachable.

Once you have renamed your documents to show how you want to organize them, you will hit the button, "New Section," on the page, which is located on the top right corner. This creates your first section. Now, you hit "Bulk Upload" and select all the files and documents that you included in "Section 1," regardless of what format they are in. When you do this, the files in question will be uploaded as their own, separate sections. Once Section 1 is ready, you can hit "New Section" again and repeat the whole process, but this time for Section 2. You can keep going until your entire curriculum is uploaded.

The process of uploading content on Teachable and thus creating new courses is fairly simple, as you can see. But this is not the only benefit of using Teachable. In fact, there are many advantages to Teachable, starting with the fact that their conversation rate tends to be very high. Another advantage is that they are known for their customer support service. Perhaps this is why their employees offer courses on how to navigate the Teachable platform and do various things, like uploading materials and customizing pages, for instance. So, if you ever feel lost when working on your Teachable page, you can easily write to customer service or check out the many articles, videos, and blog posts that may prove helpful to you.

Other benefits the platform has to offer include:

- A built-in payment system, which handles transactions on behalf of its instructors.

- A built-in marketing system that enables instructors to reach out directly to students.

- Monthly payment options for expensive courses.

But like any platform, Teachable comes with certain disadvantages as well, like:

- The fact that it does not have a free plan.

- How its customization options for courses and schools are limited.

- How their tech support team can only be contacted via email.

- How they do not have a marketplace for you to take advantage of.

Still, Teachable has various features that online instructors can make great use of. For instance, the platform **actively manages enrollment** on instructors' behalf. This means that it keeps track of who is enrolling in your courses on your dashboard. Not only that, but it also shows what lessons which students have taken and how far along a course they are.

The platform also makes it possible for you to **create quizzes**. These quizzes feature multiple-choice answers and are usually very easy to prepare. On top of that, the platform has a **built-in email service** that makes reaching out to your students very easy and vice versa.

Podia

Another platform you could use to launch your online courses is Podia. Podia has been around since 2014 and so, is another veteran of the industry. The courses you create on Podia are, again, referred to as products, at least by the platform itself. As expected, you will first have to open up a basic account on Podia, before you can think about creating your course. To begin this process, you have to click on your avatar on the upper right corner of the page and enter your information, like your full name, the name of your site—your courses will appear on your site, after all—and upload a logo of your site, if you have one. The ideal size for this logo is 200 x 60 px.

Once done, the platform usually has you move on to setting up your payment method. For this, you either need to have a PayPal account or a Stripe account. You have to click on "Payments" and then click on the account you want to connect to Podia, then enter the necessary information in. When that is done, it will be time to create your product, that is to say, your course. To that end, you need to click on the "Products" button on the top menu. Next, you need to hit "Create First Product," which takes you to a new page. You have to enter your course's name on this page. After that, you will be able to move on to uploading your content. Doing so requires selecting the kind of content you would like to upload from the section entitled "Product Editor." Once there, you have to choose between the following options:

- Add Text

- Add Link

- Add Quiz

- Choose File

If you click "Choose File" you will be able to upload any kind of file onto the platform from your computer, tablet or smartphone. Basically, you can keep adding files in this manner until all of your content has been moved to the platform. All that will be left to do afterward will be to click "Publish," located on the upper right corner of your screen.

The process does not end with uploading your content though. Next, you are required to design and build your homepage, which luckily is not all that complicated. Your home page is the place where you tell your audience about yourself and your courses. It is also obviously, where your courses are displayed.

So, to build your home page, you have to click on your avatar on the upper right corner of the page, access "Site Editor," then press "Edit Site." Doing so will take you to another page where you can find three design templates and a blank website design to choose from. These options will appear to you as:

- blank site

- email lander

- link Page

- full website

Unless you have actually had someone design a website for you, the option you want to go with is "full website." When you click on it, you are taken to your website, replete with all the courses you published. Now, if you want to change things like the order in which your courses are displayed, you can do so by clicking on the "Products" tab on the top menu. This will take you to your "Products" page, where your courses will be displayed. There, you can click on the "edit page" button displayed next to a course. This will enable you to edit your courses further.

One advantage of Podia is that it allows you to build an email list and thus collect subscriptions. Another is that it comes with built-in analytics and optimization tools, which can be found on the analytics dashboard. Other advantages that go with Podia are:

- Built-in e-commerce features.

- Instructive webinars.

- Affiliate marketing services.

- Live chat customer support.

- An Upsells feature.

- Ability to add quizzes.

- Ability to offer coupons to prospective students.

- Building a community with the community feature of the platform.

- Easy customer messaging system.

- Ability to integrate other apps such as Zoom and YouTube Live into your course.

Podia does have cons of its own though, including:

- Limited customization options.

- The fact that it does not come with a mobile app.

- Not having any advanced features to take advantage of.

Thinkific

A third platform you can use to start your online course is Thinkific. It was founded by two brothers, Greg and Matt Smith, who wanted to be able to reach more people across the world with their LSAT course. Their course took off and became a huge hit, so much so that business people and entrepreneurs began reaching out to them, asking how they might start their own courses as well. The brothers received so many similar queries, in fact, that starting Thinkific seemed like the most logical step to take, once they teamed up with co-founders Miranda Lievers and Matt Payne.

Thinkific was quick to gain widespread recognition after that and part of this is due to how simple the process of starting a course is on the platform. It all begins by clicking on "Get Started for Free" on Thinkific's website. Once you do that, you are taken to a page where you enter your email address, full name, and last name and choose your password. When done, you are taken to another page where you are asked to name your school and the questions "Are you already teaching online?" and "Do you already have a following or email list?" You are asked these questions because Thinkific allows you to transport an existing online course onto the platform, which is just one of the advantages it offers to users.

Next, you are expected to choose your brand color, specify which industry you will be teaching in and express how much course material you have so far. It is alright if you do not have any at this stage, though it is advisable that you prepare your course material before you start working on your course—more on that later. The following page has you enter your bio and instructor photo, which you do not have to share if you do not want to. Lastly, you declare how many people are part of your school—it could just be you or it could be more than 1,000 people. Once you have done that, you are all set and will have created your account.

Now that you have an instructor account, you can move on to actually creating your courses. This process is very simple as well. You begin by clicking on the "Start Building" button, which will appear under the heading "Add content to your course." This will take you to your customization options, where you can add your course or school logo, which is referred to as your branding on Thinkific. Once that is finished, you will go to your admin dashboard. Yet again, there will be a menu on the left-hand side of the screen, with the following items on it:

- Manage Learning Content
- Design Your Site
- Market & Sell
- Advanced Reporting
- Support Your Students
- Settings
- "Your Name's" Account
- Upgrade
- My Training
- Help Center
- Updates

You want to click on "Manage Your Content," which is at the very top of your list. This will open up more options on the list, which will read as:

- Courses
- Categories
- Instructors
- Video Library
- Share Revenue

You want to click on "Courses" now. This takes you to a page where all your courses and course bundles—which are packages of multiple courses sold together—will be. If you haven't opened up a course here yet, then this page will be empty. But there will be a "Create New Course" button on it, which you need to click. Once you do, you are given four options to choose from. These options are "blank," "pre-sell," "mini course," and "flagship course." The blank option gives you an empty page to work with, whereas pre-sell makes creating a landing page and waitlist for your course possible. Mini course is, well, a mini course, whereas the flagship course is the full course you want to publish in your school.

Let's say you clicked on "Flagship Course," so that you could work with the template that the platform provides you with, rather than build it from scratch. As always, you firstly name your course. That takes you to your coursebuilder. There are seven tabs on this page:

- Curriculum
- Bulk import
- Settings
- Drip
- Pricing
- After purchase
- Publish

The curriculum tab is where you build out your curriculum. On Thinkific, courses are made up of different chapters and each chapter has a set of lessons in them. To create a chapter, you go to the curriculum tab, click on "Add Chapter" and name said chapter. You can, of course, name your chapters whatever you want. You can call them Lectures, for instance, or Sections or anything else that comes to your mind.

Once you have created all the chapters making up a course, you have to fill them up with content. To do this, click on "Bulk Import" which will take you to a page where all those chapters you just created are listed. Those chapters will each have a button underneath them saying "Add Lesson." These lessons fall into one of three categories:

presentation, practice, and assessment. You will designate what each lesson you are uploading in a chapter is. If you are uncertain which kind of content, falls into which category, here's a handy chart you can use as a cheat sheet, so to speak:

Presentation	Practice	Assessment
Video	Downloadable Files	Surveys
Multimedia	Lesson Discussion	Quizzes
Text	Assignments	Alternative Quiz Types
PDF		Brillium Exams
Audio		
Narrated Presentation		
Webinar or Live Stream		
Articulate Storyline & HTML		

We will take a closer look at all these different "lessons," that is to say course materials in the following chapter. For now, to add a lesson, you go to the chapter you want to fill out, click "Add Lesson," choose what the lesson type is, give a title or name to it, add your content, and click save.

So, you have created all your chapters and filled them all out accordingly. You are done, right? Not quite. There are a couple of other tabs on your account page, as you will remember. The first of these tabs is "Drip." Drip stands for drip schedule, which allows you to schedule and control when your students will be able access the content you have created. You can use this, for instance, to launch a lesson or chapter at a specific date and time or even to limit how many lessons a student can access in a chapter, at a given time. You can determine these things by taking a look at when students have enrolled for a course, when they started it and what the date is. By using this information, you can tailor your courses so that each student gets their own, unique schedule, rather than try to follow a pre-set one that may or may not work with their day-to-day activities and programs.

Another tab on your account page is "Pricing." This lets you set pricing options for your courses, which can range from subscription/membership to free, one-time payment and monthly payment plan. Lastly, there is the "After Purchase" tab, which allows you to customize your course, chapter and lesson pages to your specifications. Once you are satisfied with the page, you can click on "Publish" and voilaé! Your course is now accessible to students interested in taking it.

As with all of these platforms, Thinkific comes with certain pros and cons, The pros can be summed up as follows:

- Thinkific is known to increase course revenues.

- It allows course creators to create quality content very quickly.

- It has a simple and easy admin interface.

- It makes scaling courses and schools easy.

As for the cons, they merit some consideration as well:

- The landing pages can be hard to build, comparatively speaking.

- Thinkafic does not have live chat customer support.

- The designs for blocks used for page building are limited.

- It has limited integration options for other apps and platforms, like ClickFunnels.

Kajabi

Kajabi is one of the oldest platforms you can use to build your online courses. That does not mean that it is out of date, though. It simply means it is a veteran of the industry. Kajabi was founded in 2010, to serve instructors, whom it referred to as "knowledge entrepreneurs". As of January 2023, Kajabi is operational in over 120 countries, serving some 60 million students, as its CEO Ahad Khan stated. Kajabi is not just good for creating online courses though. It is also used to create podcasts, coaching programs, memberships and communities, by many.

As before, you need to create an account on Kajabi before you can move onto creating your course. You can do this by entering your essential information, like your name, surname and email address and choosing your password. That done, you will be taken to your dashboard, where you will find the tabs you need to create your website—where your courses will be displayed—and your products, meaning your courses. Before you can build your courses, you have to craft your website.

The good thing about Kajabi is that it provides you with ready-to-use templates when crafting your website. All you will have to do is add your copy—the text you have written, such as a paragraph describing your course, for instance. When you first click on "Website" on your dashboard, you will see that Kajabi has laid out all the essential pages you need for your school, such as your logic page or your course library. To start, you choose a design template for your main website, fill it out with text and customize it if you'd like. The customization process is quite simple as all your options are laid out neatly for you to try and choose from. You move through your various pages in this manner, until they are ready to go. After you have done that, you can head over to the "Products" tab, where you can create your courses.

Once again, Kajabi provides you with various templates to choose from as you build your courses and how they'll look on a web page. There are two types of courses you can create on Kajabi: mini courses and full courses. To create a mini course, you have to click on the "New Product" button on the upper right corner of the page in the Products tab. This will take you to a page filled with the following options:

- Blank, which can be used to build a course from scratch.

- Mini course, which can be used to create shorter courses.

- Online course, which is good for creating a full course.

- Drip course, which is for creating a series of courses.

- Membership, which you can click on to create a membership system for your students.

- Coaching program, which you can choose if you'd rather do online coaching.

- Community, which you can use to build out an online community.

If you want to build a mini course, you will have to hit the "Get Started" button below it, which will open up a window for you. You can write the course name, course description and add a thumbnail for it on this window. Click on "Submit" once you have done all that and you will be taken to a page where the skeleton of your mini course will be waiting for you. This skeleton will consist of pre-generated course contents, listed as "Lesson 1," "Lesson 2" and so on. There are three lessons on this skeleton, but you can add more to it by clicking the "Add Content" button on the page.

To fill out these lessons, you have to click on them and open up their blueprint so to speak. There, you will be able to add any written text, video, image, audio, assessment and text onto the lesson. You can upload all this material directly from your computer and fill the text boxes you see with writing. Once you have filled up the lesson, you can click preview to see how it will look once your course is launched. If you are satisfied with how your lesson looks, you will click "Publish" which will make it live and thus accessible to students. The same logic applies to building actual courses. The only real difference between the two is their length, because a full course will, obviously, have more content in it than a mini course.

All that being said, what are the pros and cons of starting an online course on Kajabi? The pros of the platform are easy to see and can be listed as follows:

- It is good for hosting multiple different kinds of content and programs.

- It has a great system that can be used to assess student progress.

- It makes developing courses a very simple process.

- It makes developing sales pages quite easy to do.

The cons, on the other hand, are:

- It is that the page builder takes longer to navigate than those of other, similar platforms.

- It makes branding and customization a bit difficult.

- It needs to have better onboarding mechanisms, as the existent ones fall short of those of similar platforms.

LearnDash

Founded in 2013, LearnDash is an online learning platform that many colleges and universities have taken to using since the pandemic. As such, it lends itself particularly well to academic courses. It is also good for entrepreneurs who are looking to share their knowledge, designers who want to share their skills with others and training organizations that want to make training easier and more accessible to new employees.

To start using LearnDash you have to open up an account as an instructor. This is as simple as registering to the platform using your email address, which takes you to your very own WordPress dashboard. The dashboard will have a menu on the left hand side of the screen, which will read as follows:

- Overview

- Courses

- Lessons

- Topics

- Quizzes

- Questions

- Certificates

- Groups

- Challenge Exams

- Coupons

- Assignments

- Reports

- Add–Ons

- Settings

The overview section here contains helpful videos that you can use when trying to figure out how to create courses and publish them or even how to sell them. To create your first course, click "Courses" in this dashboard menu. This takes you to a page with three tabs on it: All courses, Settings, and Shortcodes. In the "All Courses" tab, there is an "Add New" button. This is what you need to press to start building your course. Pressing this button will take you to your page builder, where you have to write down your course title, followed by your course content.

Once you have written the basics, click the "Builder" tab, which is next to "Course Page." This is what you use to add lessons, topics, section headings and the like to your course. Think of your section headings as simple titles summing up a set of lessons that are grouped together. Start by creating a section heading first, then click "Add New Lesson" below it. Once you do, you can enter the lesson's name and press enter. That done, you can click on the tiny arrow to the right of the lesson title, which will give you the options "Add New Topic" and "Add New Quiz." If you choose the former, you, again, have to write down the topic's name.

Once you have entered the names and titles of all the sections, lessons and topics, you click on "Lesson" located in the menu on the left hand side of the screen, so that you can start filling them out. When you click on this, you will find all the headings you have created for your lessons displayed neatly before you in an organized list. To add content to a lesson, you click on it to open up its page. The page that opens up will now provide you with a blank space that you can add any kind of content to, including videos, images and text. After you have added all your content to a lesson, through a simple "click and upload" process, you can go to the "Settings" tab on the same page to determine things like when students can access a lesson and how long a video will be shown for on the page students will see and add lesson materials. You can also use this segment to upload assignments students have to complete after the lesson.

The process of building courses is fairly easy, as you might have gathered from what we said so far. But this is not the only advantage that comes with using this platform. There are others:

- Organizing courses is very easy to do using the drag and drop feature that is found in such WordPress plug-ins.

- Videos are easy to integrate into lessons because LearnDash has a videos feature.

- LearnDash also has a drip feed option, which gives instructors the ability to space out their courses however they'd like.

- Various functions on LearnDash can be automated using third-party plugins and apps such as Zapier.

- The LearnDash software actually allows you to create content in different languages, which makes this a very good option for instructors who either want to teach in a different language or teach foreign languages to their students.

As expected, there are various cons that come with the platform as well:

- You cannot use LearnDash if you do not have a WordPress website or application. Hence, you need to get one first.

- LearnDash does not come across as all that user-friendly to those that are new to WordPress, which makes it a little difficult to use.

- In keeping with that, the LearnDash team does not provide users with enough tutorials, which causes them to struggle even more.

- If you want to actually make money off of your courses, you will have to get apps like Woocommerce and then learn how to use them, seeing as LearnDash does not help with this.

Given these pros and cons, it can be said that LearnDash might not be the best for newcomers, at least not ones who do not have some idea how to use WordPress. However, it does give users a lot of customization options and is easy to use once you learn. So, it can be a great option for those instructors who are willing to brave the steep learning curve that might come with it.

Udemy

The final platform you can use to create and launch your online course is Udemy. Like Kajabi, Udemy is one of the veterans of the online courses industry, seeing as it was founded in 2010. As of December 2022, it accommodated over 57 million learners, more than 74,000 instructors, offered at least 213,000 different courses and had 773 million course enrollments. One of the reasons that Udemy boasts such figures is that it is available in 75 languages. This means that it is used on a global scale. It also means it is kind of perfect for teaching foreign languages to students.

To create your Udemy instructor account, you need to provide the platform with your email address. You also need to provide them with either your PayPal or Payoneer account, if you are going to be a paid member, as opposed to a free one. The first step to doing this is clicking on "Teach on Udemy" on the Udemy page and then on "Become an Instructor." This takes you to a page where you are expected to answer some questions about your previous teaching experience. Once you complete this survey, you are taken to your instructor dashboard, where you can set up your profile. Here, you have to provide Udemy and your future students with the following information:

- Your instructor name.

- Your headline, meaning your specialization or occupation, which will be related to what you will be teaching your students.

- Your professional biography.

- Your primary language.

- Any links to other websites you'd like to share.

- Your profile picture.

You can create your first course on Udemy, after you have completed your instructor profile. Having grown accustomed to the general process by now, it should not surprise you to know you have to use the course builder to create your course. To start, go to the Udemy homepage and click on Instructor, which will take you to your "Courses" page. Once there, you can click on "New Course." The page that opens up when you do this has a menu on the left hand side, with the following items on it:

- **Plan your course.**

- Intended learners.

- Course structure.

- Setup and test video.

- **Create your content.**

- Film and edit.

- Curriculum.

- Captions.

- **Publish your course.**

- Course landing page.

- Pricing.

- Promotions.

- Course messages.

You use this menu to upload different parts of your course. When you click on "Intended Learners" for instance, you are given a page that asks you some questions. The first question you are asked is "What will students learn in your course?" In other words, you put in the learning objectives you long since determined. That done, you tackle the next question, which is "What are the requirements and prerequisites for taking your course?" The one after that is "Who is this course for?" If you could not tell, filling out the "Intended Learners" section is something you can easily accomplish, after you have finished working on your syllabus.

Next, you are to click on "Curriculum" on the left-hand side menu. This is what you use to structure your course. That means this is what you use to upload your content. You can accomplish this by using "Bulk Upload" and uploading all the content that goes with a lesson or course you are building. Once you are done, you can click on "Captions" to add in the closed captions of the videos you are using. Though this is an optional step, it is one you really should do, seeing as there is no guarantee a student of yours will not be hearing impaired.

Meanwhile, you can click on the "Course Landing Page" to write your course title, subtitle and course description, as well as provide other basic information about it, such as what language it is in.

Having said all that, what are the overall pros and cons of Udemy? The platform actually has an abundance of pros, which can be summed up as follows:

- Udemy is one of the more affordable online teaching platforms out there.

- It offers close to 600 free courses to students.

- It has a 30-day refund policy.

- It makes building a syllabus a much simpler process.

- It is incredibly easy to use.

- It is available in a myriad of different languages.

- It has a lot of support services, including courses you can sign up for free explaining how to create courses.

- It has a great community of instructors that not only can interact with one another but often offer active support and advice to one another.

All that, however, does not mean that Udemy is not without certain cons:

- Udemy is a very competitive marketplace, with its own search engine. This search engine lists instructors based rankings, reviews and ratings when students search for keywords related to the courses they teach.

- Udemy unfortunately does not allow for personal branding.

- Udemy does not work very well for niche categories like beauty, arts and gardening, though does work splendidly for categories such as business, programming, technology and marketing.

- It is hard to generate a lot of revenue on Udemy, as courses are typically priced around $10, meaning you'd have to make 1,000 sales per month to be able to make a living using solely your online courses. This can be rather challenging if you are new to making such courses.

Given these facts, Udemy might not be the best for beginners, that is if you were hoping to immediately make a lot of money. It can be a good option to consider, though, if you are thinking more long term, because earning a decent income on Udemy is certainly possible. Just ask Joe Parrys, who made $500,000 on the platform by teaching things like cryptocurrency and programming languages.

But again, do not expect this to be immediately the case for you when you first launch your online course, be it on Udemy or another platform. Your success as an online instructor will depend on three things: the quality of the content that you generate, how in-demand it is and your marketing strategy. The importance of finding your niche to identify an in demand field that plenty of people will want to know more about has already been covered, of course. But what about your content? How can you create top-quality content that will appeal to and engage students? Perhaps even more importantly, how do you go about creating content to upload on these various platforms anyways?

Checklist

	Determine your reasons for wanting to offer an online course
	Identify the platform that suits your needs

Chapter 4:
Creating Your Content

There are several different kinds of content you can create for your online course, as you might have guessed by now. There are video tutorials, which are an essential part of online lessons. There are narrated presentations and texts that you can make use of. There are video clips and PDFs, articulated storylines and surveys, quizzes, and exams, to say nothing of all the assignments you will be giving. If you want your online course to be successful and reach a lot of students, then you have to put careful thought into each one of these things. You need to be diligent and creative in creating your content, so that you can craft engaging and entertaining materials which will keep your readers hooked. How, precisely, can you achieve this then?

Creating Online Lectures That People Will Actually Watch

Online lectures are a huge part of course content. They are the primary way you deliver the information that your students have signed up to receive. As such, they have to be both well-researched and actually interesting. Your online lectures have to be well-researched if you want your students to actually acquire the knowledge or skills that they want. It will also need to be interesting if you want to hold their attention long enough for them to be able to learn something.

There are two kinds of online lectures that you will typically deliver in an online course: video tutorials and narrated presentations. Video tutorials are videos of you explaining various concepts and ideas, showing how to do things, and demonstrating various experiments. These, in turn, can be divided into even more categories. Video tutorials, for instance, can be divided into talking head videos and how-to videos. The same goes for narrated presentations, which can be divided into screen capture videos and animated videos. Screen capture videos are recordings that display something on your screen, such as your presentation, and have you talk over them. Animated videos, on the other hand, are videos featuring dynamic, animated visuals.

Regardless of what kind of video you will be creating for your online course, the first question you need to ask yourself is, "Who is this content for?" You have to consider your students' needs if you are going to create a recording that will actually meet them. You also have to ask yourself what they will find engaging. If your students are going to be a bunch of 12-year-olds learning math, for instance, their needs and the things that will keep them engaged will be very different from those of seniors learning how to garden or 20-year-old bachelors learning basic cooking skills. You will additionally have to consider what the goal your students want to achieve at the end of your course is. In other words, you will need to remind yourself of your course goal and learning objectives as you prepare course materials like video recordings.

Storyboards and Scripts

Now that you have gone over your students' needs, profiles, and goals, you will need to create a basic storyboard and script for your video. Creating a storyboard is a good idea because it can help you keep your videos short, clear, and interesting. If your video ends up being long, it can also help you to segment it. Segmenting long videos and keeping your videos short overall is a good idea, as you will remember, given your audience's short attention span.

To start your storyboard, take out a pen and a piece of paper and write down what the key objective of your video is. Then write down its key messages and determine how long it is going to be. Next, gather all the information that you will be conveying in this video and organize it into chunks. If you were making a video about making a three-layer chocolate cake, for instance, you would organize the information as:

- The ingredients you need for cake and frosting.

- Making the cake.

- Making the frosting.

- Assembling the cake and the frosting.

Once you have organized the information in this manner, you can start thinking about diving into steps and putting them in a simple storyboard. Quick sketches and stick figures would serve you perfectly well as you did this.

Once you have a logical, easy-to-follow storyboard in your hands, you can start working on your script. Having a script to work off, will make you more confident as you go about creating your video and help you to be more organized. It can ensure you do not forget to deliver any essential information to your students either. The good thing about a video script is that it does not have to be overly long, just as it does not have to be overly detailed. You are not writing something for Hollywood, after all. It just needs to lay out the information you will be conveying in your video thoroughly and efficiently. To that end, you can use this simple format as you work on your script:

Voiceover	Action

Recording

Finally, once your script is complete, you will be able to move on to the recording phase. Of course, there are a couple of things you should watch out for, that is if you want to make sure your video is interesting and engaging for your students. For starters, you should avoid any and all jargon if you can. Holding online courses means not being able to see and directly interact with your students, at certain points. In other words, it means not knowing who exactly is listening to you as you speak. If a student is not a native English speaker, then your use of jargon can confuse and alienate them. It can become a barrier to them, preventing them from really getting into your video. The same can be said for students who are new to a subject. If you are using complicated terms, assuming all your students will be familiar with them, despite teaching a beginner's course, then odds are, you are going to end up alienating a number of your students.

While you are at it, you should also try to keep your sentences short and concise. You should be as clear as you can be, taking care to speak slowly and enunciate properly too. If you are using sentences that spin on like yarn unspooling and if you are talking so fast that understanding your words becomes a challenge for your students, then your students are not going to stick with your course for very long. Why should they, when they can't really get what you are saying?

In keeping with that logic, you should also try to explain complicated concepts and ideas in simple ways and with plenty of illustrative examples. That way you can capture the attention of a kindergarten teacher, for instance, as you are talking about quantum physics. You can also prevent someone with no crypto or trading knowledge, who is trying to learn about cryptocurrency to figure out how they should invest by listening to your lecture, from slipping through the cracks.

A key thing to keep in mind when recording videos is to make sure you do not sound monotonous. Sounding like this would be a sure way of boring your audience to death. Think of it like this: would you rather listen to someone talk in a robotic voice that can put you to sleep or would you rather listen to someone who is clearly very excited about the subject they are talking about? Which would pique your curiosity more? Which would you be more likely to stick with?

Finally, if you are filming a video tutorial where you are visible, try to use descriptive hand gestures, as much as you can. Social psychologists refer to such hand gestures as "co-speech gestures". They have observed that using co-speech gestures get audiences more engaged. Co-speech gestures help audiences—in this case, students absorb and internalize the messages associated with them quicker. In other words, using co-speech gestures in your videos would not only get your student more interested in what you are teaching, but they would also improve their ability to learn.

Engage Your Students

A sure way to make any video more engaging and entertaining is to add interactive elements to it. These will change up the format of your video, adding an element of novelty to it. They will also get your students to be a little more active, rather than remain passive observers. Breaking up your videos and adding exercises into those periods in between, for instance, would be one way of doing this. Another would be providing students with interactive video quizzes. Interactive quizzes basically embed multiple-choice questions that students and learners can answer in the middle of on-going videos. They literally pause the video, until the students watching answer the question and only then does the recording continue. This video is a lot more interesting and engaging for the students, while giving them a quick opportunity to review what they have just learned. A number of the platforms we have seen offer this feature to their instructors. Those that do not, however, can use video software, such as Screenflow—which will be covered momentarily—to create such in-video quizzes.

Other interactive video elements that instructors could take advantage of are in-video animations and interesting transitions between different scenes. These work particularly well in narrated presentations. Speaking of, there are some rules to creating engaging and interesting narrated presentations as well. The first and most obvious one is to prepare well and get organized before you start working on your presentation. This can mean printing out each of the slides that make up your presentation and either preparing note cards or short, separate scripts for them. This way, you will know exactly what to say when a particular slide rolls around.

Another key rule to creating a good narrated presentation is to use incomplete sentences, in bullet-point format in them. That might sound odd, but think about it: would students be more likely to read a full paragraph that you paste onto a slide or a handful of bullet-points that they can easily breeze over? On the whole, try to spend only a minute, at most two, on each slide. This will keep your video from going on for too long and it will keep your audience's attention from wandering mid-slide and mid-presentation.

Keep your audience's attention span in mind as you work on your slides and try to communicate what information you can use informational visuals—meaning graphs, charts, and other such interactive elements, which make your presentation more interesting—where you can. The key word there, is "informational." You should avoid using purely decorative graphics as much as you can, because they can be both distracting and take an unnecessary amount of time.

That does not mean, however, that you should not use an attention-grabbing design overall. To the contrary, you should, while being careful that you do not prioritize style over substance, of course. Choose a good font, but not one that is more beautiful than it is legible. In fact, try to use the same font throughout the entire presentation. Pick three colors to use in the entire presentation and stick with them and only them. Capitalize only what's necessary and only make the things you really want to stress **bold**.

As you are narrating your presentation, be sure that you are actually talking to your students, rather than reading to them. This goes back to what we said about sounding excited, interested in, and engaged with the materials you are sharing with your audience. Conveying emotions like this would be a bit difficult when you are reading facts from your note cards.

Make an effort to engage with your students. Ask them questions in your videos, even if they cannot answer you at that moment. Give illustrative examples and even tell short anecdotes and stories that are relevant to what you are talking about. In doing so, you can turn your subject matter from an abstract concept into a visible narrative.

Filming and Editing

Finally, ask yourself the following questions while recording your videos, regardless of what type of video they are. In doing so, you can adjust your narrative style, pacing, and more, depending on your answers, and make your video into something that is actually pleasant and informative to watch:

- Am I being as clear as I possibly can be? Are the instructions I am giving to the point?

- Do my explanations, ideas, and slides flow seamlessly from one to the next?

- Mentally speaking, how strained is my audience at this moment? Should I lighten the load a little bit, keep going, or up the ante a little?

- How is my pace? Should I slow down, keep going as I am, or speed up a little?

- What is my tone like? Is it friendly and approachable, robotic and monotone, or something else? Should I change it?

- How is my content coming across right now? Has it gotten a little too narrow or is it able to speak to a broad audience at this moment?

- Is my narration, video, or presentation polished enough?

If you are preparing recorded materials for an online course, then you will need to have certain equipment. To start, you are obviously going to need some kind of recording device. When you are filming a video tutorial or recording a narrated presentation, you need to make sure that the resulting video is of good quality. If you are using your computer to record yourself, this will mean using software like Camtasia or Screenflow. Both these software can be used when you are recording yourself or when you are recording your screen and therefore your presentation, while you are narrating it in the background.

Camtasia is a very popular software among online course instructors, because it can work on both Mac and Windows computers. Screenflow, on other hand, can only work on Mac. Hence, if you have something like a Dell or Casper, you will have to use Camtasia. This is not the only reason why Camtasia is popular among online course instructors, of course. There is also the fact that it offers users a massive video template library to choose from, makes audio and video editing possible, allows for full–screen, partial, and multi-screen recording, has an audio library filled with royalty-free soundtracks, gives you the ability to create interactive quizzes in videos, has different transitions and animations and permits you to integrate PowerPoint presentations into videos.

If you have a Mac, though, you might give some serious consideration to Screenflow instead. This is because the software has some very interesting features such as video editing, video annotations, zooming options, the ability to record a screen and use camera recording at the same time, a massive stock library filled with various videos and images, as well as a lot of transitions, animations, and image overlays. Screenflow also has the ability to filter out any unwanted background noises, which can be immensely helpful.

Video software is not the only thing you will need to have on hand when you are preparing video tutorials and narrated presentations. Other things you will need to give some serious consideration to are your recording device, lighting situation, and audio recording capabilities. If you have decided to film your video tutorials using your smartphone, you should use its main camera, rather than the one in front which you would use to take selfies. As a general rule, the main camera of your phone will be better quality than the front one. To properly film yourself, using either your phone or an external camera, you will need a good tripod and a clamp so that you can hold it in place. This way, you will be able to avoid shaky camera syndrome.

As for audio, you may want to consider investing in a decent microphone, which you can get on Amazon for around $47. The Rode smartLav+ Lavalier Mic, for instance, would be a safe bet to go for, especially since it can be plugged directly into the headphone jack of your phone or computer. Getting a mic for recording purposes is a must, because it improves the audio quality of your videos significantly.

If you do not want to use your phone or a camera for recording purposes, you can use your laptop instead. You should make sure that your computer has a good quality webcam and, if not, consider investing in another one. You can easily find one in your price range on Amazon. Keep in mind, however, that even the best camera in the world will not be able to do much for you if you record your video tutorial in bad lighting. For optimal lighting, you should try to record your videos on either completely sunny or completely overcast days and position yourself close to the window so that you can take advantage of the natural light.

Once you have recorded your videos, you can move on to editing them and polishing them up a bit, using software like Camtasia or Screenflow. You can edit your video content in several ways, such as:

- Adding raw materials in.

- Mixing sound.

- Adding closed captioning.

- Editing the footage.

One of the biggest challenges instructors face when it comes to editing the videos they've made is not having any extra content or media to work with. This extra content, otherwise referred to as raw material, could be anything from a photo or an image to another video clip and even audio clips you'd like to use. It is important that you know which raw material you want to use in your videos and where to roughly place them, so that you can edit them in later. If you were teaching an online course about world history, for instance, one of your raw materials could be a world map. You can insert this map into relevant points of your video, but you can only do that if you have already chosen which map or image you want to use.

Raw materials are an important part of the editing phase, as is mixing sound. Mixing sound involves doing things like reducing or eliminating background noise, adding background music, and adjusting the volume of your video. Doing such things can both make your content more engaging—dramatic music does have that effect on people when used correctly—and more understandable. Adding closed captioning to videos can have this latter effect as well. This is especially true if you have an usual accent or in the case of students who are hearing impaired.

As for actually editing footage… This is basically the process of cutting out bits of video footage that you are not happy with and then pasting the remaining footage back together. This probably sounds like a very difficult thing to do, but honestly, it is not. At least, not in this day and age, where software like Camtasia and Screenflow are available to all. These two are not the only software you can use to edit your footage, though. You can also use Adobe Premiere and Final Cut Pro. If all you really need to do is cut and paste some footage, you can even use free and simple tools like QuickTime and Movie Maker. For more complicated tasks, though, you will have to turn to one of the four, aforementioned software out there.

Regardless of which software you are using though, the process of editing them will basically be the same. You start by opening up a program. For argument's sake, let's say that you have gone with Camtasia. Once Camtasia is running, you upload your media, meaning your video, any images you want to use, and your audio recording on it. Your media thus appears in your "media bin.". Next, you drag the video you want to work on below, to the area called the "timeline."

After your video appears on your timeline, you can click on it. A very small thumbnail of it will appear on the lower right corner of the blank, black screen at the center of the program. When it does, you can click on the thumbnail and drag it to the center of that screen, where you can make it bigger. Having made that image as big as you want it to be, it will be time to begin the trimming process. You can do this by selecting portions of the video, as it appears on your timeline, and clicking on the split tool to break it into chunks at the spots you want. In doing so you will have split the video footage into separate scenes. If you want to delete any of these scenes, all you have to do is click on it and then click "delete" on your keyboard. Simple as that. Once the scene disappears, you can move the preceding scene into its old place in the timeline. In doing so, you will be able to piece together your video.

Alternatively, you can leave that blank space blank and drag the image you wanted to insert into your video there. So, again, if you were teaching a world history online course, you could drop your world map image into that blank space. Once you are done clipping out scenes and inserting raw material into your video in this manner, you should watch your video at least once from top to bottom. This way you can immediately spot any mistakes you may have made or things you might have forgotten to include and fix them ASAP.

Having said that, you do not want to go from one scene to another, a seemingly unrelated one without some kind of transition. Doing so can be rather jarring for your students and mess with their concentration. Luckily, software like Camtasia comes with many different transition effects for you to choose from. Among online instructors, the two simplest and the most popular transition effects are called split edit and cross dissolve. If you are watching a video and you begin to hear the audio of the next scene, before you see its corresponding image, then you are looking at a split edit transition. If the screen darkens momentarily in the video you are watching and then a second scene appears, then you are looking at a cross-dissolve transition. If these sound a little too familiar to you, you are right. Both are techniques that have been used often enough in both various TV shows and big Hollywood movies like *Kill Bill* and *Godfather*. You can find both readily available in the effects library that your software comes with and drag them into your footage.

On top of all this, these kinds of software will grant you the use of a number of different features, which you can use to make your video content more dynamic. One such effect is known as the "lower third." The lower third is that effect that makes a small video of you appear at the lower right corner of a larger video, say of a presentation you are making. Another useful effect is called the Ken Burns effect. This is when you insert a static image, like a photo, but make the "lens" of the camera glide from one corner of it to another, making the viewer—meaning your students—think it is not actually static.

Exporting Your Files

Once you are done exploring all these cool effects and have decided that your video is ready to go, you will have to export it. This, oddly enough, is the most difficult part of the editing process, not the actual editing itself. Actually, the process is quite simple on Camtasia, but gets to be a tad difficult on other software. On Camtasia, the only thing you have to do to export your video is to click the "Share" button, then choose "Local File" and finish things up by saving your video as an mp4 file on your computer. Afterward, you will be able to upload it onto whatever platform you are using to host your course as your course or lesson content.

As I said though, the export process is not quite that simple on other software. Take Premiere Pro, for instance. On Premiere Pro you will want to save your video as an H.264 file. To do that you first have to confirm that your timeline is active, then click on "File," then on "Export," and, finally, on "Media." You then have to choose your format—again, go with H.264—and save the file on your desktop as an mp4.

Creating Assignments

Your videos and presentations are not the only materials you will have to prepare for your course. You will also have to prepare various course assignments to help your students practice what they've learned and to evaluate how well they've learned. Now, most, if not all, online teaching platforms out there allow you to upload the assignments you create onto your lessons and courses as either PDF or Word documents. Your students then download these documents to work on them. The question is not what software to use to create these assignments then—a simple word doc will suffice—nor is it how to upload them. It is how to create good, effective assignments that can actually achieve their goals.

First, there are certain guidelines you should follow, if you want to create the kind of useful assignments you ultimately want.

You can think of these as the seven commandments:

- **First and foremost, always be clear.** Make sure the assignments you create always give very clear instructions to your students and learners. Communicate the learning goals that your students will achieved by completing these assignments. Make sure they understand the expected learning outcomes, so they can tackle the assignments correctly and without losing any time.

- **Divide long assignments into smaller, interconnected ones**. Make these smaller assignments build on top of one another and thus lead the students to their learning goals. This will help students keep expanding on their existing pool of knowledge. It will also be easier for them, because continuing an ongoing project is, objectively speaking, easier to do than starting a whole new project, once you have finished the old one. Segmenting assignments in this way has the added benefit of working with students' short attention span, thereby guaranteeing that they stay focused on their work for longer periods of time and with fewer issues.

- **Choose flexible timelines for your assignments**. This will make it easier for your students to meet the deadlines that you give them. It will make it possible for them to work on their assignments without having to rush or stress, which will lead to their getting better grades.

- **Allow students to share drafts with you before the actual assignment**. You can set draft deadlines for this. This way, you can give your students feedback and thus greater direction, ensuring that they do well in your course. This is particularly important for essay assignments and other, long-length projects.

- **Meet with your students to discuss assignments**. In other words, have virtual office hours or email sessions where you can talk to your students about assignments and give them any clarification and help they need. Be sure to be available both before important assignments and after them as well.

- **Have a learning management system in place for students to work on their assignments**. A learning management system is a system that helps students to improve their performance through discussion and collaboration. A message board, for instance, where they can ask questions about assignments or brainstorm about ideas, is an example of a learning management system. So is a feature that allows students to upload drafts of their work and give each other feedback, comments, and ask questions to one another to better their work.

- **Use technologies that you are comfortable using and make sure your students know how to use them, before giving an assignment involving them.** Don't create an assignment until you are sure you know how to use the technology. Give yourself enough time to learn and familiarize yourself with the system you are using. Similarly, make sure to give your students the time they need to achieve this as well. Upload tutorial videos or provide links to tutorial videos explaining how a certain kind of app, software, or technology can be used, if an assignment you are giving out involves them.

Now that you know what to keep in mind when you are creating assignments for your online course, let's consider what kinds of assignments you can create. After all, there are a great many options to choose from, like:

- Brainstorming activities.

- Storyboarding.

- Concept maps.

- Virtual field trips.

- Online discussion or debate.

- Online presentation.

- Book reports.

- Collaborative worksheets.

- Designing posters.

- Analyzing case studies.

- Writing essays.

- Creating timelines.

- Whiteboard.

These are just some examples of the kinds of assignments you can give out, but they are very useful ones. Brainstorming activities, for instance, can be a great way to get your students to think outside the box, use their critical thinking and creative thinking skills to solve various problems and apply concepts they learn to real-life scenarios. They can also be a great way of making connections between bits of knowledge that might have appeared to be unconnected at first.

Giving your students **brainstorming assignments** begins with posing them a question or presenting them with a problem that is related to the topic you have been discussing in class. You can have students work individually on these problems or team up, thereby turning them into group projects. Encourage your students to use techniques like **mind mapping** when they are brainstorming.

Mind maps are a visual technique students can use to organize their thoughts, knowledge, and ideas. To create one your students have to identify the starting point of the map, which will likely be the topic or problem the assignment is having them consider. They express this topic or problem using a single keyword or symbol and place it at the very center of their map. Then, they come with ideas, themes, solutions, answers, and subjects that may be related to it, as well as ones that are related to the keywords that branch out from the center word. They draw connections between these different words and in doing so they map them out. They keep going until the map is complete.

Brainstorming activities like mind mapping can be great assignments in and of themselves, but they can also be solid starting points for research projects, essays, and presentations. This means that you can give your students a brainstorming activity assignment for one class and then ask them to turn that assignment into an essay, research project, or something similar in another. In this way, you can have assignments feed into each other and support one another. This is just one of the advantages of brainstorming activities, though. Another is that these kinds of activities are very simple to do. Your students can literally draw them by hand and submit a good-resolution photo of their drawing. They can also draw them on a Word Doc or PowerPoint slide and submit that to you instead. If you want, you can even find free-to-use brainstorming and mind mapping templates that you can share with your students, as PDFs.

Assignment Ideas

Concept mapping is a similar assignment to mind mapping, in that it is an activity that can illustrate the connections between different concepts and ideas. To begin the process, a student has to write down the key concept or idea that is under discussion. This is the starting point of the map. They then do a quick brainstorming session to identify linked themes, concepts, facts, and the like. Next, they start drawing their map, except they position their key concept at the very top, rather than the center, the way they would in mind mapping. From there, they'd move downward and outward and link the key concept to main themes and concepts with linking phrases, such as "consist of," "helps get," "is illustrated by" and "can be done," to name but a few examples. Main keys and concepts would then be linked to other, related concepts, thoughts, ideas, and more. Again, like mind mapping exercises, concept mapping is a great stand-alone activity, as well as a starting point for bigger projects like presentations, research papers, and more.

Storyboarding, which you already know how to do if you have used it when working on your video tutorials, can be a great way of keeping track of narratives. They can be handed out assignments for creative writing courses or even science courses, as the first step to planning an experiment that can prove or disprove a theory or hypothesis that has been explored in class. They can be an excellent tool to gauge how well students have understood a concept you have been covering in your lessons. If you are giving your students storyboarding assignments, you need to give thorough guidelines that they could use to create one. You should both go over these guidelines in class and include them in the assignment instructions. If you want, you can provide your students with a simple template they can use to storyboard, which you can easily find online for free.

Another similarly creative assignment you can give out is to have your students prepare comic strips. This is a particularly good assignment to give for drawing classes, though it can be used in many other fields of study as well, such as foreign language courses, English as a second language courses, history classes, and creative writing classes. Obviously, if your online course is not about drawing and drawing skills, you should not grade comic strips on how well they are drawn. It should not make a difference whether the characters populating the strip are stick figures or proper characters, with shading and all. Instead, you should read these strips and try to see how well your students have understood the concepts you have been discussing and what knowledge gaps you still need to fill. Your students can hand-draw comic strips, scan or take good-quality photos of them and then send them to you. Alternatively, they could use a free app like Synfig, which is a 2D animation software that is easy to use for beginners. If you go with this latter option for this assignment, though, you should thoroughly explain how to use it in class, provide tutorial videos that you have either made or found for your students and provide thorough written guidelines.

Seeing as physical field trips are not exactly a possibility for most online courses, **virtual field trips** are a good substitute for them, one that you can dole out as an assignment. Typically, all you have to do to give this assignment is to provide a link for the virtual place you want your students to explore. Let us say you are teaching an online art history class. A great many museums across the globe create virtual renderings of their physical galleries, which people can visit from the comfort of their own homes. This means that you can ask your students to take a virtual tour of the Van Gogh Museum in Amsterdam, for instance, without having to go to Amsterdam. You can take this assignment a step further by asking your students to write **reflection papers** about their trip. Such papers could focus on their overall experience and what their favorite piece of art at the museum was. It could even focus on the concept of virtual tours and how they compare to physical ones.

Once you are done thoroughly exploring an idea, theory, or concept in class, you can give your students **case studies** that illustrate it. One assignment might be to **read these case studies and be prepared to discuss them** and what they prove or exemplify in class. Another is to **write a paper on it**. Still, another way is to **prepare a presentation** for it and to make that presentation to the rest of the class. Of course, for this latter assignment to work, you would need to assign a different case study to each student or group—this may be a group project too—so that they do not all present the same things. Alternatively, you can **ask your students to find good case studies showing what you have discussed** and bring them to class. This could be a very interesting research project for them. If you are teaching a course on social psychology, for instance, and you have just finished going over the phenomenon known as groupthink, you can ask your students to find examples of it. Your students would then take to their computers and the library to find cases from historic protests or even cults that might be illustrative of how groupthink works and affects groups.

Giving your students a case study to examine is just one way of starting an **online discussion or debate**. Another is to pair students together and assign one subject to every two groups. One of the groups could discuss the pros of that subject. In other words, they could defend it in the upcoming class. The other could discuss the subject's cons. This way, the two groups' assignments would be to prepare well for their upcoming debate and then to conduct their online debate when it is their turn.

Whiteboard teaching is a method that has students take a concept and explain and teach it to their peers. It is a well-known fact that one of the best ways of learning is by teaching. This is one of the reasons why study groups exist after all. Giving out a whiteboard teaching assignment requires that you assign each student in your course a subject, topic or concept. The student will then have to research that subject and prepare a presentation on it. They can then make that presentation to their peers in your next course and explain their subject to them as clearly and thoroughly as they can. Ideally, you should give each student a set period of time to finish their presentation. Otherwise, they might go on for too long, preventing you from ending class on time, or keep their presentation too short, resulting in no one gaining a decent understanding of the subject in question.

Book presentations are great assignment options for foreign language courses, English as a second language course, literature and creative writing classes, history lessons, and more. If you are going to have your students do book presentations, then you must make sure that the books you are assigning them are easily accessible. Ideally, this means providing them with downloadable PDF or ePub versions of the books you have chosen. If you are assigning all your students the same book, then you can have them present on different aspects of it. One, for instance, can present the protagonist's character development in the book. Another could present on the book's main theme, while someone presents on how the historical time period that the book takes place in is represented in the story. Similarly, you can assign your students various topics about the book and have them **prepare posters** illustrating and explaining those topics. Such a project can help them gain a better understanding of the theme in question. Of course, poster projects are not just good for analyzing books. They can be great for examining scientific concepts covered in class, explaining cryptocurrency trends, taking a closer look at historical periods, and more. Put simply, poster projects can help your students understand a variety of subjects better by thinking carefully on how they could explain and visually represent them.

Timeline projects are a kind of visual tool that can make for very handy assignments. They can be very useful when studying specific time periods, the period of time that certain experiments or processes take, and can be good alternatives for written narratives. They have the added benefit of not taking as long as say, an essay would, to write, and of becoming an outline for future essays. A simple timeline involves a long, straight line with dates or times written on one side of it and the events that correspond to them on the other. Your students can prepare such timelines by hand and send you scanned versions of them or make them in a Word Doc and email them to you. You could also find blank timeline templates online and give them to your students.

Collaborative worksheets make for great group projects. To create one all you have to do is open up a Google Doc and create a worksheet on it. This worksheet can be filled with all manner of questions, like multiple-choice ones, fill-in-the-blanks, comparisons, true and false statements, and more. Once your worksheet is ready, you can share the Google Doc it is on with your students. Your students can then answer the questions in it and you can, in turn, give them feedback, greater direction, and comments.

To create an easy-to-follow and effective worksheet you need to follow certain guidelines, as you might have guessed. Otherwise, you might end up providing your students with an assignment that is difficult to understand and therefore finish. You will also make the grading phase infinitely more difficult for yourself. These guidelines can be summed up as follows:

- Make sure that there is a place at the very top of the worksheet where your students can enter their names. Otherwise, you will not know whose work you are evaluating.

- Keep your instructions concise, clear, and straightforward.

- Place the learning objectives and goals of each assignment, question, or task at the top.

- Stick to simple and clear language, especially when explaining what an assignment is asking a student to do.

- Stick to using action verbs while you are at it.

Building Activities

Building activities are another kind of assignment you can hand out to your students. They can be especially good for courses that are about developing different skills, such as cooking or DIY projects. Essentially, you can give your students something to build or create, tell them which ingredients or materials they are allowed to use, and tell them to figure out how to accomplish their task based on what they've learned. For instance, if you are teaching an online course about engineering or architecture, you could ask your students to build a functioning bridge out of spaghetti and paper. Alternatively, you can also give your students directions to follow. You can ask them to make a chicken cordon bleu, for example, and film themselves making it, along with what the end result looks like, and then send that video to you.

Finally, you can have your students **interview** various people as part of their assignments. This can be a great assignment for, say, history students, journalism students, or for a media course. Students can film themselves interviewing family members and friends and send you their videos. It could also be part of a larger assignment such as a research project.

Once you have created your assignments and once your students have finished and handed them in, you will have to undertake the troublesome task of evaluating them. If you have assigned worksheets to your students with, say, multiple-choice answers, this grading process will be fairly simple. After all, your students will have either chosen the right answer or the wrong one. Grading other types of assignments, however, is a little more complicated than this. Regardless of what kind of assignment you are grading, there is one question you have to ask yourself: did the student demonstrate that they really understood what was taught while completing this assignment? In other words, you have to look at whether or not they met the learning objective of the assignment in question.

Evaluating Assignments

When you are evaluating assignments, then, you must begin by going over what the learning objective there was. Was it to see if they had been able to develop a certain skill you'd been teaching? Was it to see how well they understood a scientific or mathematical concept? Was it to gauge their understanding of a historical time period or a book? Grade assignments bearing these questions in mind. Once you are done going over an assignment, provide your students with positive feedback. That does not mean do not remark on the things they have forgotten or gotten wrong. On the contrary, you should point these things out. You are giving out assignments so that students practice what they learn and you see where they need more help with, after all. It does mean, however, you should word such things in positive, encouraging ways. For example, you should remark on things they can improve upon, while also highlighting the things they have done well. This way both the student and you will get a full, clear picture of their overall progress, which means that your student will be able to tackle their weaker points with greater enthusiasm and you will be better able to provide them with the support that they need.

Fairly and objectively evaluating your students' progress is essential for helping them to improve and get the most out of the course that you are teaching. Being able to do this, though, is naturally dependent on you actually having students. Without students, you will neither be able to evaluate any work nor start making the passive income you want. So, how do you get students to enroll in your class? How do you let the people that you are targeting know that there is now a fantastic course designed to help them? Keep reading to find out.

Checklist

	Create a storyboard for each lesson
	Write a script for each lesson
	Start recording your lessons
	Create additional engaging and interactive content for your students
	Edit your lessons to ensure they are engaging and professional
	Export your edited files
	Create assignments and activities
	Evaluate your assignments

Chapter 5:
Getting the Word Out There With Online Marketing

The online courses market is a rather competitive space. According to one report published in 2021, approximately 220 million students had taken at least one online course between 2012 and 2021. The same report showed that over 950 universities had launched over 19,400 online courses since 2012 as well. Making your online course stand out and attract the students you want, then, can be a bit of a challenge. However, it is not impossible to do, at least not with the right marketing strategies in place.

Creating a Marketing Plan

The first step to any good marketing strategy is finding a good niche to exploit in the marketplace. Hopefully, you have now done that and created an excellent online course to go with it. Now, come the next steps of your strategy and this begins with creating an effective marketing plan. Your marketing plan is a document that outlines the steps you will take to market your online course and puts them into a logical order. There are two kinds of marketing plans: product launch–based ones and social media marketing plans.

For now, let us focus on your product launch-based plan, rather than your social media plan, though we will get to that shortly as well. A marketing plan is actually quite easy to write, especially since there are numerous, free-to-use templates out there that you can take advantage of. Regardless of what template you use, your marketing plan essentially consists of five sections:

- Your value proposition.

- Your key performance indicators (KPIs).

- Your target market section.

- Your strategy and execution section.

- Your budget.

Your value proposition is the overall value that your course expects to deliver to your students. It is the statement that answers the question "Why should I choose your online course?". It should identify what factors set your course apart from your competition and what student problems it helps to solve. Your KPIs, on the other hand, are the measures you will use to measure how successful your marketing plan is. A good example of a KPI is how many people end up signing up for your course and how that figure changes over time.

Your target market section tackles the group you are targeting for your online course. Since you already will have explored this group when working on your niche, this section will be easy to write. You can use the student profile you had created, for instance, in this section, outlining general things like their age group, sex, and interests. This is also the section where you explore what their needs are in a little more detail and how your course will meet those needs.

Your strategy and execution section covers the methods and techniques you will use to find the right students for your course and convert them into loyal followers. This can be anything and everything from advertisements to newsletters. Finally, your budget section will determine what kind of budget you will devote to these methods and techniques.

One thing you should keep in mind when you are working on your marketing plan is that you should be flexible. This means being open to making changes to your plan if you observe that a certain method you have been using is not working, for instance. This is crucial to the success of your marketing efforts.

Seeing as the product you are trying to sell is an online course and considering the kind of world we live in today, the bulk of your marketing efforts will focus on online marketing strategies. So, what kinds of methods and techniques can you use to properly market your online course?

The first thing you need to do to properly market your online course is to **create a good landing page** for your courses. Your designated landing page is where you feature your courses, introduce who you are, and explain why students want to take your course. It is your introduction to the wider world. It is how you announce upcoming classes, as well as any other news relevant to your courses. Having a good landing page can help you create anticipation for a course, before it is released and convince prospective students to give your course a chance. To do this, your landing page has to focus on your value proposition. In other words, it needs to explain what students will gain by taking your course. This means that you should not just focus on talking about *what* you will be teaching your students. You should also primarily focus on *how* the thing you are teaching will help them. A good strategy to adopt, where your landing page is concerned, is to feature incentives like promotions and various discounts on it. This can make more hesitant or skeptical students more likely to sign up for your course.

Aside from a landing page, you will obviously also have pages for your course. These pages should feature glowing **reviews from your previous students**. These should not be generic reviews that do not go beyond stating your course was "just awesome." Instead, they should go into some detail about what your students really liked about your course and what they gained from it. These reviews, then, should demonstrate how prospective students can benefit from taking your course.

Another method you can turn to is the **power of SEO**. SEO stands for "search engine optimization" and it can be a great way of driving more traffic and, therefore, students to your landing page. If you are teaching a course on herb gardening, for instance, you want to use SEO for the words "herb gardening" and any related keywords. This way you can make sure that your course is one of the first options to pop up when someone is doing a google search for those words. This can be incredibly effective, as 91.74% of search traffic to a given site is driven by google searches. To properly use the power of SEO, you need to **identify popular keywords** relevant to the course you are teaching, which you already discovered how to do in previous chapters. If you need even more resources to identify more keywords, though, you can always use Google Keyword Planner, Ahrefs, Keywords Sheeter, Keywords Everywhere, and Answer the Public.

You then have to make sure you use those keywords on your landing page, as well as your other web pages. If you can, try to put a keyword in your course title, the URL for that course, and the headings and subheadings found on the course page. Repeat your keywords several times in the texts that are featured on your course page. Highlight these keywords or even key phrases by making them bold or italicize them.

A great way to make sure an online course turns into a passive income source is to **publish some of the content it covers as an eBook** that you can then make available on Amazon. The good thing about eBooks is that they are quite cheap. They are also very easy to publish in this day and age, especially through platforms such as Amazon. So, people must not hesitate to buy them, the way they might with a hardcover book, especially if it is on a subject that they want to learn more about. When publishing your course content as an eBook, you should make sure that you do not use all of your course material in the text. Instead, you should give just enough information to get people interested and to educate them a little. You should then mention that readers who want to know more about the specifics or details of certain subjects can take a look at your online course. As an added incentive, you can put a promo code of some kind in your book that your readers can use to get a discount when signing up for your course.

Remember how a number of online teaching platforms allowed you to prepare mini courses? Well, these **mini courses** can be a great marketing tool as well. Your mini courses can thus become bite-sized versions of your full courses. You can make them either cheaper than your full courses or offer them up as free, though the latter would be a better strategy to adopt. They can thus serve as hooks that can reel in students who try them, like the content you offer, and want to learn more. Doing **a live webinar every once in a while** that shares some of the key information you discuss in your course with your audience can serve as such a hook too. Webinars typically run for about 45 to 60 minutes. As such, you could not share all the information that your course, which is made up of multiple lessons, in your one, even if you wanted to. You can, however, cherry-pick the most interesting and relevant ones and share them with your audience at your webinar, whose date and time you should announce in advance. That way you can pique your audience's curiosity, get them more intrigued and drive them toward your course after your webinar.

You might have heard of the term "**content marketing**" before. This is a marketing technique that uses things like blog posts to generate interest in various brands and products. Mattress companies, for instance, write blog posts about how a good night's sleep improves the immune system and cognitive functioning, then link that back to the importance of having a good mattress for a good night's sleep and ultimately try to get customers to buy their product. The same logic can easily be applied to online courses in one of two ways. Either you can **start a blog** that links to the landing page for your courses or school or you can **act as a guest blogger** on various websites and blogs. You can also do both of these things simultaneously. Blog posts are an excellent way of increasing student enrollment because they effectively demonstrate your expertise in the subject you are teaching. They make your prospective students curious about the things you have to share with them and, therefore, more likely to take your course. If you are maintaining your own blog, you should definitely make sure that you use the power of SEO keyword optimization in your blog posts. That way you can reach more people through google searches. If you are acting as a guest blogger, you should try to write for as many good-quality blogs as possible. Try to choose ones that are relevant to the field you are teaching a course on and with a wide following.

One easily overlooked marketing strategy is **working with other online instructors** to promote your course. This can be as simple as having a Zoom chat to understand one another's courses and then mentioning it to your students and having that instructor do the same for their students. This way you can support one another's teaching endeavors. For the best results, you should collaborate with instructors who are teaching courses about subjects that are tangential to yours. After all, if an instructor teaching a course on geometry were to suddenly start directing their students to an Aerobics at Home course, that would raise some eyebrows. If on the other hand, they were to direct their students toward an architecture course, which is something that does rely heavily on geometry, as well as mathematics, then that would be perfectly understandable and reasonable. As for where you might find such instructors, one of the benefits of using online teaching platforms is that they host a lot of instructors and provide them with a virtual space that they can use to communicate with one another. In other words, they come equipped with a virtual community that you can freely take advantage of.

A very obvious marketing strategy, on the other hand, is using **online advertisements**. You might be skeptical about how well advertisements really work, thinking that not a lot of people pay attention to them. But you would be wrong seeing as even a $10 Facebook ad can go a long way to get you more students. The great thing about online ads is that they do not have to cost you a great deal of money. The best online ad services to use to promote your online course are either Facebook ads or Google Ads (or even both). This is because they make it easy for you to keep track of how many people see your ads, and how many actually click on them and then get converted into students. It is also because they can help you a lot of students very quickly by reaching a staggering number of people and targeting the right people—meaning the audience you were going after anyways—thereby getting you the right students.

To really enjoy these benefits though, you have to properly research the ad platform you are going to be using, give careful consideration to the overall budget you will be dedicating to your ads, and make sure the audience you want to reach actually uses the platform you are advertising on. If you are teaching a course that is targeting seniors, for instance, and they do not use Facebook all that much, then your conversion rate is going to be pretty low, no matter how good your ads are.

A final marketing strategy you can use is offering commissions to publishers to review your course. There are a number of platforms, publications and blogs out there with solid followings that you can reach out to ask that they review your course. You can offer these platforms and publications a commission from the revenue you receive from the students they direct to you in exchange for such positive reviews. After all, this can help you generate a lot of revenue really quickly, meaning that paying such a commission will not hurt you much. At the same time, this strategy, which is actually a part of affiliate marketing, can create a lot of awareness about both your course and the topic you are focusing on.

If you would like to learn more about Affiliate Marketing, why not take a look at our book, *Affiliate Marketing Mastery: The Ultimate Guide to Starting Your Online Business and Earning Passive Income.*

Social Media Marketing for Online Courses

As you may have noticed, the marketing strategies covered so far were curiously devoid of any mention of social media. This is because social media marketing is a category in and of itself and the strategies that are associated with it should be treated as such. The key social media platforms you will be using for this type of marketing are Facebook, X, YouTube, and Instagram, which you probably already use on a daily basis.

There are many, many things you can do to market your online course on these platforms. The first thing you have to do though is to **create a good promo video** for your course and launch it on YouTube. Currently, YouTube is the second most used search engine in the world, after Google. Consider just how many people must be looking up tutorials and how-to videos to accomplish all manner of things, from solving an equation to fixing a dishwasher and to writing a screenplay. This is something that you can easily take advantage of by creating a short video describing the benefits that your course has to offer to its students.

Of course, to do this, you have to first **start a YouTube channel** for your courses or school. This is a simple enough process that you can finish in a matter of minutes, by simply going to YouTube and filling out your information. When starting a channel, you should use your school's or course's name as your channel title, rather than your own name. When uploading your videos onto your channel, you should make sure to give them interesting, curiosity-evoking titles that encompass what your course is about. You should refrain from clickbait titles, though, as they can turn off your audience really quickly. While you are at it, you should **use SEO in your titles, video, and channel descriptions and even in your recorded videos** as well. To identify the right keywords to use in your YouTube videos you can turn to tools like keywordtool.io. To make your promo video even more visible on YouTube, you should select a category for it and add tags to it, which you can easily do while uploading it onto the site.

Once you have created your YouTube channel and started uploading your promo videos, you should make an effort to **engage with the YouTube community**. This includes fellow content creators on the site, meaning other people who have their own channels. You can like and comment on these individuals' videos, as well as reach out to them and collaborate with them. You can make joint videos every once in a while, for instance, or give one another shoutouts in your videos to direct your subscribers each other's way.

Now, when you are uploading your videos onto your YouTube channel, you need to **include a link to your course or website in the descriptions** you write for them. That way people who watch your videos or subscribe to your channels can quickly click on the link and sign up for your course. You'd be surprised at how many potential students you could miss out on if you do not make going to your website as easy as pressing a single link.

A good promo video is not just something you can put on YouTube, of course, You can also publish it on Facebook, X, and Instagram. Make sure you research the best hashtags to tag your video with on X and Instagram and post it with them. You do not just have to use Instagram and Facebook to post videos and images, though. You can make things a little more interactive and thus engaging by hosting live video sessions on them as well. You can announce these sessions well in advance to generate some publicity for them, thereby ensuring more people will turn up. You can use these live sessions to hold "mini courses" that cover small portions of the larger course that you are offering to your students. After you are done, you can hold Q&A

sessions with your audience and direct them to your course if they want to know more about the field you have been covering. You can take these Q&A sessions a step further by hosting "Ask Me Anything" sessions in your Instagram Stories. Ideally, you'd want to do this on the Instagram page you create for your courses.

If you would like to learn more about YouTube, why not take a look at our book, *YouTube Influencer: The Ultimate Guide to YouTube success, content creation and monetisation strategies.*

Speaking of Instagram, you should absolutely create an Instagram, X, and Facebook page for your courses or school. The description for these pages must include a link to your courses to make it easy for your prospective students to sign up for them. You must then regularly share content on these pages. Regularly typically means, at least once a day. You can start by sharing your promo videos on them, but do not have to confine yourself to such videos. There are many different things you can share on your course's social media accounts, after all, such as, but not limited to:

- Student testimonials.

- Course reviews.

- Mini-tips related to the course you are teaching.

- Resources that you use inside your course.

- Interesting visuals that you use in your course materials.

- Special offers and discounts that are given to your followers for limited times only.

- Quotes from blog posts you write.

- Video snippets from joint videos you make with other instructors.

- Content like drawings, gifs, or animations you have created, if you are teaching a course about how to make such things.

- Infographics.

The success of your social media marketing strategy in part depends on how well you use the community you discover there. This is why you need to follow and engage with people and accounts that are in the same field as you. That means you need to like and comment on their posts, tag people in your posts, and even DM people to start a conversation with them. Social media is all about building community, when you think about it and community can be a vital tool for both getting the word out about your course and creating a loyal follower base for it, as you will soon see.

Checklist

	Create a marketing plan
	Create a website with a good landing page
	Identify keywords and optimize your content for search engine ranking (SEO)
	Collect reviews from previous students
	Create and publish an ebook with some of your course content
	Start a blog or guest write on other websites and blogs
	Use social media and online advertising to get the word out

Chapter 6:
Building a Community Around Your Online Course

For all their benefits and advantages, online courses are things that both students and instructors tackle in isolation. You do not go to a physical classroom or lecture hall to attend one. You go to a virtual space. You do not sit next to your peers or in front of a professor but alone in your room or living room. At best, you sit down at a cafe or library, with your headphones in, listening to a recorded lecture, trying to learn. While this is a very convenient thing for most students, it can also be quite isolating. This does not mean creating a community around an online course is impossible though. It is, in fact, quite possible, even if that community looks a bit different than the one you'd find in a physical course or workshop you could attend.

Not only is building a community possible where online courses are concerned, but it is also vital for the longevity of that course. The plain fact of the matter is, an online course that is not able to build a community around itself will not survive for very long. So, how can you go about forming a community around your online course? How can you infuse your students with a sense of community and take advantage of the community that the online teaching world offers to you, as an instructor?

Why Community Building Matters

Before taking a look at *how* you can build a community around your online course, let's better understand *why* you need to begin with, starting with the most obvious reason: you need to build a community around your course because building a community means building a network. A single individual that is part of your community is also a part of other communities. They are a part of other networks, whose members they can easily direct your way by extolling your course's virtues. In this sense, you consider community building a kind of marketing strategy in and of itself. It is something that can spread the word about what you are doing by word of mouth and from ear to ear. That may not sound like much, but you'd be surprised at how many people it can help you reach. Especially since the cycle does not end with that one member of your community telling someone else about your course. That someone shares your course with another person as well, once they've entered your community, and then that person tells another... Before you know it, there is a bit of a wave effect going on and who would not want to take advantage of that?

Another great thing about communities is that they can help you to learn a variety of things and thus improve upon your product, that is to say your course. Members of your community will often reach out to you to give constructive feedback, as well as praise. This feedback can be invaluable. For instance, it can grant you perspectives you had never considered before. You can then take those perspectives and use them to strengthen various aspects of your course. It can grant you the distance you need to see flaws or lacks that you hadn't seen before and either erase them or fill them up. The people that make up your community who reach out to you in this way are all individuals that like your course and want to contribute something to it. They want to add to it because they consider it theirs to some extent as well and want to see it live a long life. Just as you do.

On top of all that, communities are known to support one another. The platforms that you would typically use to launch your online course host a lot of other online instructors as well. While you might consider some of these instructors your "competition" so to speak, you will find that you can build a community with a great many of them more often than not. This is a great resource to make use of, especially if you are launching your first-ever online course. Whatever platform you use, it will typically have some feature that enables you to talk to other instructors, as well as the platform's support team. You can turn to the members of this community for whatever kind of help you may need. Maybe you have a question about how to use a specific technology or software you need to make your course a success. Maybe you are looking for some marketing tips or new case studies you can share with your students. Maybe you want to team up with another instructor in a similar field and do a joint video or Q&A session with them, thereby bringing attention to both your courses.

The members of your community could help you in all these matters and more, if you simply turn to them and let them. The thing though, this support system works both ways. That means that sometimes different community members could reach out to you. Alternatively, they might post a question on the communal messaging channel you and your fellow instructors use, and you might find that you know the answer to their question. It is important that you respond and reach back out in these cases. It is important that you pay the support and help your community has given you forward. The only way to ensure that a community continues into perpetuity is through reciprocity, after all.

The reasons why you should build an online community only keep increasing the more you look at it. There is the fact, for instance, that online communities can help you be perceived as a leader in your area by expanding your sphere of influence. There is the fact that they can be a nearly effortless way to acquire your very own brand ambassadors. There is the fact that online communities can help you stay abreast of current developments in your field and quickly incorporate them into your courses, ensuring that they remain current as well. Really, the benefits seem rather endless when you sit down to think about it.

It bears mentioning that community building is not just important on a business-level, though. It is important on an individual level as well. Studies show that communities reduce the sense of isolation and loneliness that individuals—such as those creating online courses by themselves, alone in their apartments—can feel. It can help people feel more connected to the people around them, which can in turn significantly reduce their stress and anxiety levels. Reduced stress and anxiety levels typically mean reduced risk factors for conditions like heart disease that are often linked to these kinds of conditions. It also means lower odds of developing a mental health condition, such as depression. Given all this, it can legitimately be argued that community building is essential for your physical and mental health and well-being, just as it is for the well-being and longevity of your work.

How to Build a Community With Online Courses

The question, then, is not whether it is worth it to build a community around your online course or school. It is how you go about building a strong one. As an online course instructor, you want to build a learning-based community. A learning-based community is structured around the course you are teaching. It is made up of people with similar learning goals, meaning your students, who get together to discuss their assignments and course subjects. This community allows you to support your students, but it also allows your students to support one another. It increases their learning capabilities, helps them to get to the answer they want much quicker and so, results in their getting better results. This reflects very positively on your course.

One strategy you can adopt to build the learning-based community you need is to create an effective communication plan. Communication can be called the cornerstone of any community because communities are built through the formation of individual relationships. Given that, it is vital that you work to build individual relationships with your students. You can start by making an effort to get to know your students more personally, one-on-one. This way you can come to understand things like how they learn. You can also give your students the opportunity they need to come to you if and when they do not understand a particular concept or problem. This can happen through virtual chat channels where they can talk with you in private, office hours made with video apps like Zoom or emails. Whatever method of communication you use, the importance of keeping communication lines open cannot be overstated. Obviously, you do not have to drop everything and respond to an email a student sends at 3 am. But you can set aside certain times of the week, announce them as your virtual office hours and invite your students to reach out to you.

Constructive Communication

If you notice that a student's underperforming, based on their assignments, grades, and course attendance levels, for instance, you can reach out to them to check in with them and ask to arrange a call. Rather than reprimand them in these cases, you should try to uncover the root of the issue at hand and see if you can come up with a solution together. Sometimes, even making an effort in this regard can be enough to strengthen your connection with a student and thus turn them into a true member of your community and a champion of your course.

Another strategy you can employ when building an online community is to establish and then strengthen a social presence. Your social presence is that sense your students get that they are talking and interacting with a real human being rather than some bot or algorithm somewhere. If you have a strong social presence, then that means you make your students and community members feel that you are genuine. This makes them more willing to keep engaging with you, which is what you want. If you have a weak social presence, on the other hand, your students and community members feel disingenuous and end up distancing themselves from you and, therefore, your course.

Building a strong social presence is dependent on two factors: immediacy and intimacy. Immediacy is the perceived psychological distance between two people who are trying to communicate. Put simply, it is how much two different people can understand one another as they speak. Think about it: You would neither feel very close nor connected to an instructor who did not understand where you were coming from when you told them about a problem you were having, now would you? Intimacy, on the other hand, is the sense two people have that they are willing to modify and adjust their behaviors if the other requires it. In other words, it is knowing that your instructor would make an effort to help accommodate you, if you went up to them and told them something they did or that happened in the lesson really bothered them.

Communicating a true sense of immediacy and intimacy seems a little more challenging to do in a virtual learning environment, as opposed to a physical one. But, yet again, it is not impossible to do. One way to achieve this might be to create an introductory video where you share a couple of interesting facts about yourself. Since communication is a two-way street, you can take this a step further and have your students film similar videos and share them with you and their peers. This may even be one of the first assignments you give and serve as an ice–breaker, of sorts. Another way to do this could be to keep an online messaging board, where students can freely discuss anything, from assignments to their thoughts on the latest book they read, together. Of course, for this to work properly, you need to set certain ground rules for your messaging board. To that end you could:

- Have a zero-tolerance policy for harassment and discrimination, as you want both your message board and your course to be a safe, welcoming space for all your students.

- Set specific, clearly stated rules about what can and can't be discussed in the message boards.

- How members are expected to conduct themselves when they are communicating with one another on these boards and where the line between "passionately arguing for an idea you believe in during a debate" and "being inappropriate or unprofessional" is drawn.

- How the admins of the message board and moderators of discussions and debates are expected to conduct themselves.

- What steps should students and members take if and when they need to lodge a complaint about someone's behavior.

Intersocial Interaction

For a community to be robust, its different members need to be able to interact with one another. Given that simple fact, it is important that you create collaboration opportunities for your students. To that end, you can assign group projects to your students periodically. You can also create study groups. Your students can easily use the learning management systems and tools you provide them with as part of your course to be able to do and partake in these study sessions. In doing so, they can help each other understand difficult concepts that they may be struggling with and, in the process, form firm connections and even friendships.

You can further get students to keep interacting with one another by having them share interesting resources that are relevant to the subjects they are learning with one another. Students can post the videos, articles, or blog post links and images they find on the message board or even a Facebook group you open up for your course members. While you are at it, you might consider giving students interactive assignments that would require working together in groups or at least pairs to finish. Group presentations, where each member of the group is in charge of a different part of the presentation, is a great example of this. One of the simplest and easiest ways to create a community, though, is to establish a membership or subscription system for students who partake in your courses. Make sure that you have an email newsletter system in place that is regularly sent out to any and all course members. Include announcements about your course, interesting developments regarding the field it is related to, as well as news about fellow members' accomplishments. If you are teaching an online course about coding, for instance, and one student who began their coding career with your course went on to land an amazing job later on and let you know about it. That is a great bit of news to include in your newsletter, with their permission, naturally. In doing this, you will not only have celebrated the achievement of one of your members, but you will also have highlighted a success story that is associated with your course.

How Community Building Helps Overcome Possible Challenges

Community building can be great for identifying the various struggles and challenges members and students might be having and, more importantly, for solving them. Students are unique people leading different lives and therefore experiencing equally unique problems. However, the root causes of those problems are, more often than not, similar, if not the same. Most issues that students face in their online courses are caused by:

- Technological hurdles.

- Resistance to change.

- Lack of interactivity.

- Lack of motivation.

Technological Hurdles

Technological hurdlers are probably the most common issue students encounter when trying to participate in online courses. A technical difficulty can be anything from a poor internet connection to not knowing how to use a certain app, software, or even hardware that is necessary to finish an assignment. Such problems can be incredibly disappointing, that is if you, as the instructor, do not have solutions and remedies you can offer for them. There are several solutions that you can employ to help your students overcome technological hurdles, the first being testing out any and all software, programs, and apps you want your students to use well in advance is one of them. This way you can confirm that said technology is user-friendly, even if one is a beginner. You can also be ready to answer any questions your students might pose about that technology, including how to use a certain feature. Getting such a refresher can make preparing instructional guidelines on how to use the technology in question much easier to do. You can provide your students with either written guidelines or a video tutorial explaining how to use a software or program to do their assignments. Ideally, you would do both.

What if your student's technological hurdle is that their internet quality is low or that their connection is cutting out? A workaround to this issue might be to make sure all course materials, from PDF docs to presentations and even to video tutorials are downloadable. This way your students can download their work when they have a stable internet connection, complete it offline, and submit it when they have an internet connection again. Another solution might be to give students who are dealing with such internet connectivity issues extended deadlines to complete their work. That way you can accommodate their situation and ensure they remain able to pursue the course and education they want.

Resistance to Change

Resistance to change is an issue that is often observed in students who are used to doing things in a certain way. A student, for instance, may be very used to calculating an equation one way and could resist doing it using another method, even if that latter method is objectively easier. Other students might be hesitant to keep participating in their online course, because they are very used to in-person courses and classes. A key way to break down this reticence is to focus on the benefits of the methods you are trying to introduce to your students. If a student is unwilling to use a new method for solving an equation, stressing how much easier that method is and how much time it would save them is the thing to do.

If a potential student is hesitant to try an online course, then highlighting how online courses are faster, easier to attend, and more comfortable is clearly the way to go. You can highlight these and similar benefits in your course description, any promotional videos you prepare, Q&A sessions that you do, interviews you give, reviews you collect, social media posts you share... Put simply, the best way to break down resistance to change is to communicate the reasons why change is a good idea in a clear and understandable way and keep on doing that until the message finally gets through.

Lack of Interactivity

A lack of interactivity indicates a hesitancy to interact with other people. This is quite a common issue in online learning courses, because online learning can be a solitary experience, as you have seen. For people who tend to be on the shier side, this can make online learning an isolating, even lonely experience. That, in turn, can cause them to stop and abandon their course. However, there are ways to turn online courses into more social, interactive endeavors. One is through group projects, as you might have figured. Another is study sessions, which were mentioned previously. One of the best ways to circumnavigate this problem, though, is to schedule regular meetings with students that struggle with it. These meetings can be done through any video app, such as Zoom or Google Meets. In these sessions, you can touch base with your students, listen to their struggles and try to find solutions that might work for them, together. This simple act and these short sessions can go a long way to change students' perception of your course, making it grow from a solitary experience into a communal one.

Starting small, regular group sessions might achieve a very similar result, except on a broader scale. These group sessions, which should take place at set times every week or at least every two weeks, can be great for increasing connectivity and allowing students to have more meaningful conversations. It is great that you have a 30 or 40-person course. But it would be understandably difficult to have very deep, meaningful conversations in such groups. Having them in groups of four or five, on the other hand, would be a much easier task to accomplish. These small groups could then go over the concepts that were discussed in class or examine case studies closely and start various debates about them. The conversations that bloom in these sessions can make students really engage with the subjects they are learning. They can also allow them to better understand points they had missed or found to be unclear while challenging each other's points of view and supporting one another in areas they find to be difficult.

Lack of Motivation

A final, key issue that a lot of students deal with when it comes to online learning is a lack of motivation. Online learning is great in that, they give everyone the power and ability to go at their own pace. The problem with this is that sometimes, some studies lose their motivation to continue with their coursework. Some need the stimulation that a physical class or workshop environment provides. Others need greater encouragement and the feeling that they are held accountable for their actions or inaction, as the case may be. The former can be managed with things like small group sessions and group projects. The latter calls for a more structured approach, one that makes students feel that they have to adhere to a certain schedule and that they are, in fact, accountable to others. To that end, setting a specific deadline for students to complete their course is absolutely essential. It is fine if a student watches a course lecture a day or two late. But they cannot sleep on it for several weeks. Permitting them to do so would be a sure way of losing those students who struggle with their motivation.

Another key strategy to overcome hurdles that would keep students from preserving their coursework is to work to increase the students' engagement in class. While there is no big, overarching tactic you can use for this, there are a number of smaller techniques you can use and tips you can take advantage of:

- **Be sure to always communicate clearly in your videos, course materials, and when directly interacting with students**. Being vague or hard to understand is a surefire way to frustrate students and cause them to walk away.

- **Establish routines**. Routines can be very powerful tools, in that once they are set, they become very hard to break. For instance, keep the way in which you have your students submit their work and how you provide feedback to them consistently. Don't suddenly switch to a different method or start using a new technology that they will have to learn midway through a course.

- **Recognize your students' achievements and progress**. Doing this can be extremely motivating for students. This is especially true for those individuals who show improvement after struggling with a portion of your course or a specific concept. Giving praise and credit when they are earned can make your students feel seen and accomplished, thus keeping them going.

- **Create checklists for students**. Alternatively, have your students create checklists themselves. This way you can create a greater sense of accountability between you and your students, which will help students struggling with motivation immensely.

- **Have your students fill out feedback forms**. You can do this toward the end of a course or after it is finished. Feedback forms can give you a lot of information, some that you might not have even thought of, about what you can improve and build on in your course. It can also give you insight into struggles and issues you might have overlooked and enable you to come up with solutions for them.

- **Create a Frequently Asked Questions (FAQ) page for your course website**. This way you can answer important questions your students might have, which, left unanswered, could have kept them from participating in your course. Be sure to update your FAQ page regularly. You might, for instance, end up adding a question to it that a student raises in a feedback form or during a group session.

Working on student engagement is obviously a crucial part of both overcoming problems that might arise in online courses and building communities around them. Being able to raise student engagement, though, requires having a certain set of skills that will enable you to create truly interesting content and have open, warm and constructive conversations with your students. But what kinds of skills can help you to do all that? What kinds of skills do you need to have to make your online course a resounding success? Well, to discover that, you need only turn the page...

Checklist

	Find people who have similar learning goals as you and/or your students
	Use effective and constructive communication methods to reach your students
	Build your social presence and ensure that your students can call or meet with you in-person when possible
	Create a messaging board or forum for your students to interact with one another
	Provide support channels to address tech and other issues

Chapter 7:
The Skills You Need to Start an Online Course

There are four kinds of skills that an online course instructor needs to possess if they want to be successful. These are technical skills, interpersonal skills, time management and organizational skills, and assessment skills. These four skills may seem like they are wholly separate from one another. But in truth, they work in concert throughout the various sessions and lessons that make up online courses to raise students' interest and involvement. An instructor who is able to master all four different types of skills will not only draw more and more students to their courses on a regular basis, but also get their students to really emotionally invest in what they are learning. These are the instructors that can truly infuse their students with a sense that they've found a community that they belong in and are learning something worthwhile.

You might think that accomplishing all this is a rather tall order. You would, however, be wrong, because not only is achieving all this possible, but it is also much easier than you think it is. That is, so long as you know what specific skills you need and how you need to use them.

What Technical Skills Do You Really Need?

When you think of the words "technology" and "skill" the first images to pop into your mind are probably recording devices and video editing. As you have already seen though, neither recording, nor video editing is all that hard, at least so long as you have the right equipment and software. With these, editing videos is usually a very simple process that you can do with just a few clicks of your mouse. The act of recording yourself or the screen is as well. It can be said, then, that you do not really need to be highly skilled in these two areas if you want to be a successful online course instructor. You will, however, require other technical skills, such as the ones below.

Managing Files and Folders

Managing files and folders includes activities such as saving, naming, renaming, copying, deleting, uploading, downloading, and sending those that are related to your course. You will likely be dealing with a number of files and folders once you start launching your lessons. These files include assignments you will be handing out to your students, reading materials you provide them with, drafts, second drafts, and final versions of any essays they write, presentations that you prepare, quizzes that you grade, and more.

If a student sends you multiple drafts of their essay and you ended up grading their second draft, because you mislabeled it as their final draft or did not save it where you should have, that would be problematic. Having a good file management system in place, though, can easily keep you from committing such errors. At the same time, it would improve your organizational skills. This can help you keep track of student progress through their work, assignments, quizzes, and tests. It would also make you pick up speed when sharing important files and information with your students, seeing as you would know exactly where to locate them.

That brings us to another benefit of file management skills, which is that they make centralized document location possible. A centralized document location system simply means keeping all your files in one place, organized into accurately titled folders. If you have a centralized system, you could quickly go into your main folder and identify the sub-folder you need by just glancing at its name. Then you can go into that sub-folder and find the documents you are looking for just as rapidly.

The ease that a centralized system affords you, obviously increases your efficiency, and this, in turn, improves another important skill you will need to make use of—time management. At the same time, your increased efficiency translates to better and faster communication with your students. In light of these facts, it can be argued that file management skills are one example of how your technical skills can feed into both your time management and organizational skills and your interpersonal abilities.

Software Installation for Virus Protection and Security

Knowing how to manage and install anti-virus software is another significant technical skill that course instructors should have. A virus can be defined as an unwanted program or system that, once downloaded onto your computer, can self-replicate, spread, and perform unwanted, disruptive, and even malicious actions. These actions can include accessing your students' personal information and slowing down your computer processes, thereby lowering your performance as a course instructor. Anti-virus software are programs that can protect your computer against such viruses and eliminate them from its system, if and when a virus manages to make its way past the firewall the protection program has put up.

It's easy to see why you would want to have a solid virus protection system in place as an online course instructor. This is especially true for those instructors who frequently download suggested worksheets, activities, and assignments from free-to-use websites. While many of these websites do offer legitimate course materials or templates to use, others are not quite that helpful and offer a serving-up to viruses to go with those materials. So, why take that risk or risk of downloading what you thought was an assignment a student sent in only to realize it was a virus, when protecting yourself is a simple matter of downloading the right protection program?

Anti-virus programs do not just protect you from viruses, though. They also throw up firewalls against hackers trying to access your data, prevent pop-up ads from bothering you, protect all files and documents, including your course-related ones, and safeguard your passwords. To top it all off, anti-virus programs are neither too costly nor difficult to download. As far as skills go, it is a very easy one to master, so long as you know which anti-virus software *to* download. The best antivirus software you could download are:

- McAfee Total Protection, which is very easy to set up and protects against all manners of virtual threats.

- The Norton 360 Suite, which is a top-notch virus protection program that throws in a bunch of extra features, but does come with an irritating renewal fee.

- BitDefender Total Security, which has a wide array of protective features, though some are more useful than others.

- Microsoft Defender, which works especially well on Microsoft products—such as a Microsoft Tablet, for instance, and is a free-to-use tool with excellent protective properties.

To download one of these programs, go to their website, click on "download" for the software that you want, and then run the program once it is on your desktop. So, again, as far as skills go, this is a very simple and straightforward one.

Computer Literacy

As an online course instructor, the two programs you will have to use most often are Microsoft Word and Microsoft PowerPoint. Word will serve you well when you are preparing things like worksheets, evaluating students' assignments, and reading their essays. PowerPoint is something you will have to rely on heavily when you are preparing presentations for class.

You likely already know how to use both, but let us go over the basics anyways, starting with Word. When you open up a Word Doc, you will have the option to choose from a set of templates, and to use a blank page. The template that Word offers you can actually be very useful to you, as an instructor. They can help you pick up speed, rather than lose it by having to create everything from scratch. So, take a quick look at these templates when Word first opens up, to determine which would be of most help to you.

Every time you open a Word Doc, you will find that the documents you had opened and used most recently are displayed under the heading "Recent." If you want to pick up even more speed, you can press on the Word icon to launch the program and then click a file you had been working on the other day, so that you can continue your work. You can also click on "Open Other Documents" to find a file you have been working on a while ago, thereby saving yourself minutes of search time. That might not sound like a lot, but remember that minutes ultimately add up into hours and even days of your life.

To save a document once you are finished working on it, you have to click on "File" on the upper right corner, then click "Save As" and choose where you want to save your file to. Remember to save your files in your centralized folder, which you should keep in a Cloud of some kind such as Dropbox or One Drive. This way you will be able to access your documents from any computer and will not risk losing them if you spill water on your laptop or something like that.

If you give a lot of essay assignments, then one feature you want to make use of is called "Track Changes." Track Changes allows you to make edits on the essays that your students write but keep them visible by making them read in another color. When you delete a word that a student wrote in their essay, for example, and suggest another in their place, Track Changes crosses out the word you have chosen to delete and writes the suggested replacement word next to it in a different color. To make use of this feature, you will have to click on "Review" in the menu options that are available at the top of the document and then click on "Track Changes." Once you are done making edits with this feature, you should remember to click "Save" so that the alterations you make are not lost.

What about PowerPoint, then? To create a presentation on PowerPoint you first have to launch the program. When you open PowerPoint, you can either work on a blank slideshow and create everything from scratch or you can choose a theme. Think of themes as the PowerPoint versions of templates on Word. To choose a theme, click on "File" on the upper left corner of the top menu found in PowerPoint, then select "New." This will give you four color options to choose from. You can then select the option you want and then press "Create." The slides that will make up the presentation you are working on will now exclusively be in that color.

To add new slides to your presentation, click on the "Home" tab located in the upper menu and then press the bottom half of the "New Slide" button. You can do this as many times as you need and so, use as many slides as you want. You should, again, remember to save after you have added slides, so that your progress isn't lost when you exit PowerPoint. You can do this by clicking on "File" and "Save As," the same way you would in Word.

An interesting tab you can make use of in PowerPoint is the Formatting area in the upper menu. Here, you will find text boxes of different colors, different colors you can use for your text, and even an option called "Text Effect," which will enable you to do things like shade letters. As you are adding these kinds of effects and coloring in, keep in mind that it would be best for you to keep your style uniform throughout your presentation. Otherwise, it might end up looking a bit too chaotic and thus, become distracting. If you have opted for a blue text box in your first slide, for instance, you should make sure all your text boxes, in all your slides, are the same shade of blue.

You can add pictures to your slides by clicking on the "Insert" tab and then choosing the image you want to add from your computer. Once you are satisfied with how your presentation looks and is structured, you should click save. After that, you can click "Slideshow" to see how it will look as a slideshow that your students will be taking advantage of. If you find anything to be bothersome or distracting, you can easily spot it in this mode, close the slideshow, fix the issue and press save once more. To avoid potential distractions, you should stick to the following rules when working on your presentation:

- Keep your texts short and simple.

- Use clear visuals that can quickly communicate your messages when and where you can, rather than writing oodles of text-filled lines.

- Use a legible font and make the font size at least 30, where texts are concerned.

- Use subtle colors in your slide backgrounds, so that they do not distract from the content of those slides.

- Proofread and double-check your spelling and grammar.

That last item brings us to another important technical skill, which is proofreading. You want to make sure that every single document you share with your students is grammatically correct and free of spelling mistakes. As such, you must proofread everything that you prepare. While you might be a great proofreader, you might sometimes make minor mistakes. That is understandable as you are only human. This is where the "Spell Check" feature of Word and PowerPoint comes in. To check your spelling and grammar in these programs, press the F7 key. Once you do, a spell check will be run on your work and mistakes will be highlighted in red or blue. You will be able to spot them very quickly and tend to them. If you are using a program other than Word or PowerPoint or if you want to be doubly sure of your spelling on these programs, you can always download a trusty spelling app like Grammarly. Once you do, Grammarly will run its own scan of your work and highlight mistakes you may have missed.

Using Online Communication Tools

While most of your classes will consist of things like video tutorials, knowing how to use a video chatting app is important. By becoming savvy in this area, you can communicate with your students one-on-one and go over their work with you, participate in group sessions, check in on study groups, do joint sessions with other instructors, and more. Most instructors either rely on Google Meets or Zoom for their video chatting purposes. If you already have a Gmail account, odds are you do, then that means you already have Google Meets. You can find your Google Meets app in your Gmail. To access it, open up your Gmail and click on the "nine dots making up a square" icon on the upper right corner. There you will find a video symbol. Clicking on this will take you to your Google Meets video chat room. Once there, you can click on "invite guests" and send email invitations to your students. They can then accept this invitation and start appearing in your Google Meets room, one after the other.

A very useful feature of Google Meets is the "Presentation" option. Clicking on this allows you to share your screen with your students. If you are having a live class, for instance, you will be able to pull up your course presentation for the day and share it with your students then and there. This feature can also be found in Zoom, though there it is known as "Screen Sharing." The process is similar in that you need to click on the screen share button to allow your students to view your screen. To use Zoom, you will have to download the app onto your computer, then quickly start an account using your email address and choosing a password for yourself. That done, you will be taken to the opening page of the app, so to speak, where you will have the option to start an instant meeting, join someone else's meeting, or to schedule a meeting. The process of starting an instant meeting is much the same as the process for starting one in Google Meets. To schedule a meeting, on the other hand, you have to click the right button and designate what date and time you want that meeting to be held. When you are doing that, make sure you are choosing the right time zone. If you live on the East Coast and accidentally choose 3 p.m. PST, for instance, you will likely end up missing your own, scheduled video session. Once you have scheduled a "meeting," you can send the meeting invitation to your students via email.

What Interpersonal Skills Will Help You?

Some of the technical skills you need as an online course instructor feed into and support your interpersonal skills. Your interpersonal skills are your social skills, which are a huge part of community building, an essential staple of online courses as we have seen. Your interpersonal skills play a huge role in increasing student engagement and making them feel like they belong in your course. To get a little more specific, the essential interpersonal skills you need as an instructor are:

- communication skills

- open-mindedness

- patience

- empathy

- active listening

- positive reinforcement

- self-confidence

Though the importance of communication skills has already been touched on several times throughout this book, let us do a quick recap. Communication, be it verbal or written, is vital when engaging with students. If you want to be an effective instructor, you have to make sure that you communicate as clearly as you possibly can. This means giving clear, concise, and understandable instructions. It means choosing your words consciously. It means being mindful of and illustrative and open in your body language, especially in your video tutorials. It means listening to your students and giving them the opportunity to ask any questions or raise any concerns they might have, because communication is always a two-way street.

Given that fact, patience is something that goes hand in hand with communication. The truth is, not all students learn at the same pace. Some take a longer time to digest the information that they are provided with. Others sometimes struggle with various concepts or theories that you are discussing with them. Practicing patience is crucial when interacting with such students, if you want them to keep persevering and participating in your course. This means explaining the concepts again and again, without showing any visible frustration or annoyance.

What if a student isn't grasping a concept after you have explained it to them a couple of times? You may feel like your patience is being tested at such a moment, but rather than give in to that feeling, you could re-evaluate how you are communicating with that student. Are you being as clear as you can be? Are you giving enough illustrative examples to better explain the concept you are talking about? You may also want to consider your students' learning styles. It's true that different students learn at different paces, but it is equally true that they learn in different ways. Some students learn better by doing, for instance. Others learn by listening. Still, others need to read and take notes if they want to be able to learn. Identifying your students' learning methods can help you communicate with them in the way that they need and this can, in turn, help you practice your patience.

Of course, patience requires empathy to exist. You can't really show someone patience, if you do not understand where they are coming from. Empathy is a way of doing this, as it literally makes you put yourself in other people's shoes. As such, it is something that can make you understand the specific struggles your students are facing, as well as their root causes. Understanding these can enable you to come up with effective solutions for them. More specifically, practicing and expanding your empathic abilities can help you to see things from your students' perspectives, approach various topics without a sense of judgment, comprehend your students' feelings and thoughts better, and communicate that you get all these things. Put simply, then, empathy can make you communicate more openly with your students, thereby forging stronger connections with them.

If you want to treat your students with more empathy or develop your empathic abilities, you might consider trying some of these techniques:

- **Always ask your students open-ended questions**. Don't assume that you know exactly what a student is thinking or feeling. If you do, you might miss important problems that are possibly keeping the students from participating in your course fully. In other words, you might miss out on an opportunity to understand and solve a struggle they are facing and turn them from a student who'll eventually quit the course into a brand ambassador.

- **Use "I feel" statements, when you are discussing a student's performance or behavior**. This way, you can avoid making your students feel like you are blaming them. This is important because when people feel like they are being blamed for something, they tend to get more defensive. When they get defensive, they avoid addressing the root cause of an issue and even exacerbate it. "I feel" statement, on the other hand, can be a great, constructive way of starting a dialogue with students and helping them to become more engaged in your course.

- **Validate your students' feelings**. If a student is sharing frustration with you, do not make the mistake of dismissing how they are feeling. Instead, really try to listen and understand them and, what's more, validate what they are feeling. That you might not agree with their reaction to their feelings does not mean those feelings are not real. When you validate students' feelings, you give them the recognition they need, and you create a platform where both of you can work to remedy both the situation that caused your student to get frustrated and the problematic reaction they gave to that feeling.

As you might have noticed, all these interpersonal skills are intimately connected with active listening. Active listening is the act and process of fully understanding the meaning and intent behind what a student is telling you. It's your ability to be fully present during a conversation and grasp whatever it is your student needs to communicate. Active listening, then, is something that can quickly strengthen the bond between you and your students. If you want to practice your active listening skills and get better at them, there are several techniques you can try. Some examples might be:

- Asking for feedback from your students and making a genuine effort to incorporate what you learn from that feedback into your future behavior and course.

- Repeating back issues your students bring to you or feedback that they've given you to show that you understand and asking valid questions about them.

- Having students summarize things that they've learned in that day's lesson or course, to make sure that they have been actively listening as well.

- Keeping yourself from interrupting your students when they are speaking.

- Encouraging your students as they speak, using body language by giving them nods, smiling and keeping an open posture.

The last item on this list actually falls in line with another interpersonal skill, which is giving your students encouragement. As we have seen, external encouragement can be very important for students, especially if they sometimes struggle with their motivation. But of course, positive body language isn't the only way you can encourage your students. One other way you can achieve this is to remark on the progress that your students have made when you give them feedback. It's important to point out areas of improvement, to be sure. But it is just as important to highlight students' strengths and how far they've come, if you want to encourage and motivate them too.

A final, significant interpersonal skill you want to practice is your self-confidence. Let us face it, no one would want to listen to an instructor who seemed unsure of themselves. If there is a voice inside your head that keeps saying, "No one wants to listen to me, anyway," or "Why do I even bother?" then listening to that voice will impact your mentality and the way you go about teaching your course. Your now self-doubt filled attitude will filter into your posture, your voice, the way you talk, and even how well you are able to hold eye contact with your students, that is to say the camera. Such things will give your student the sense that you are not the kind of instructor that can help them, even if you are a well-noted expert in your field.

So, how can you avoid this self-confidence trap? How can you become a more confident online instructor? You can start by choosing to teach a course on a subject that you absolutely love. This way, you will be able to communicate how you feel about that subject through your body language, tone, and words. Your passion will generally trump your hesitancy and the eagerness with which you talk about your passion will make your confidence grow. This is yet another reason why exploring your passions is so important when you are working on your niche, which we had talked about at the very start of this book, as you will recall.

Another thing you can do to give yourself a confidence boost is to do breathing exercises or mindfulness practices before filming your video tutorials or doing a live session with your students. This way, you will be able to calm down your body's stress reactions and consciously regulate your emotions and thoughts, thereby keeping imposter syndrome at bay.

A final trick to try might be to embody someone whose self-confidence you admire. Asking yourself "What would … do?" and then answering that question honestly could be a great way of putting yourself in the right frame of mind. Once you have your answers, you can think about how you can emulate those behaviors more. The more you try this technique and make an effort to accomplish, the easier it will get. It's the whole, "fake it till you make it" logic, after all.

What About Time Management and Organization?

One of the keys to creating a successful online course and not becoming overwhelmed by the work is having good time management and organizational skills. Time management is all about being organized when you think about it. It's about figuring out how long various tasks will take, putting them in an order of prioritization, and creating a schedule that works for you based on that.

This might be a hard skill to master though, especially when you are launching your first-ever online course. This is why it is important that instructors develop daily and even weekly routines. Without routines, losing track of time and overworking become all too easy to do. With routines, though, you can start putting strategies in place to deal with different kinds of work and know exactly when you should tackle them. A good way to start a routine might be to check your email or messaging channels in the mornings, to see if your students have sent you anything. Working on new video tutorials and materials for your next lesson or refining and uploading them might be something you do in the afternoon. You could conclude your routine by devoting a set period of the night, on certain days of the week, to evaluating and grading assignments, quizzes, and tests.

This is just one example of how a routine might go through. Yours might look entirely different and that is perfectly alright. It's important that you find a routine that works in the context of your day-to-day schedule and with your needs. Some people, for instance, work better in the afternoons than they do in the morning. Others do their best work early in the day or very late at night. Since online courses give you the flexibility you need to structure your time however you want, why not work with your preferences and arrange your routine and schedule accordingly?

That being said, you might still be wondering how exactly you are supposed to go about making a daily schedule for yourself. How should you prioritize your course related to-dos, for instance? How much time should you allot to each of your tasks? Start by making a list of everything course-related that you have to do that day, when you wake up in the morning. You can also make a list of everything you will have to do tomorrow or the night before. Once you have done that, ask yourself which of these tasks should be your first priority.

You can determine your priorities based on when your tasks are due and how important they are. For instance, if you are giving a quiz to your students in three days' time and have to upload a new video tutorial for your course tomorrow, then the latter task should take priority. Once you have done that, you can finish working on your quiz. What if you also have to go over the instructor evaluations that your students have given you? Well, you can tend to that after you are done preparing your quizzes. After all, the evaluations, while important, are not on a deadline and are more important in the long term than in the immediate short term. They will require a greater time of reflection and less urgency on your part. Ergo, you can finish preparing your quizzes this afternoon, and then move on to going over your student evaluations tonight.

Schedule Flexibility

When you are working on your routines, you should take care to keep your schedule as flexible as possible. To that end, you should plan for any potential crises. Let us say you have a very rigid schedule and you get sick. Therefore, you become unable to prepare your course material or evaluate your students' on the date and time you wanted to. In this case, your entire schedule might get thrown off and you may find yourself playing a lot of catch up. If you create a flexible schedule, on the other hand, where you can move things around as needed, you could save yourself a great deal of time and energy.

One thing you absolutely need to do if you want to manage your time well is to avoid "loaded" procrastination. Procrastination is the act of delaying things you have to do. Loaded procrastination is the act of piling up numerous assignments and to-dos on the same day, rather than taking care of them bit by bit, over the course of a couple of days. Let's say that you have 30 assignments to grade. If you try to do them all in a single day, you will overwork yourself and start feeling quite stressed and overwhelmed. If, however, you were to grade just five assignments per day, you could take care of the entire batch in six days. You will likely spend, at max, an hour per day on grading these assignments, which is much more manageable than spending six hours in a row trying to push through them.

An often overlooked and underappreciated time management strategy is scheduling breaks for yourself. This might sound a bit odd. You might be thinking that taking a break is the opposite of working and therefore would be counterproductive. You'd be wrong. Contrary to what some may think, breaks are not a waste of your time in any way, shape, or form. Rather, they are a way for you to prioritize and meet your personal needs. Instructors are human beings, which means they have certain needs. Truth is, no one can work indefinitely. Human beings both need bodily rest and mental rest if they are to keep functioning. Without it, they will exhaust themselves too much on both levels and become more inefficient and less productive. The quality of their work will suffer as a result, along with their mental and physical health. This will slow them down even further and make it impossible for them to put their best foot forward.

If you make a point of taking regular breaks, however, you can avoid all this. Most people who work long hours while sitting down are encouraged to take three to five-minute long breaks once every 30 minutes. They are further encouraged to take at least one longer break—at least 10 to 15 minutes long—during the day. If you worry about forgetting to take such breaks, you should schedule them into your daily plan. You can decide exactly when you are going to take your breaks, how long they are going to last, and even set yourself alarms, so that you do not lose track of time and forget. This way you can make sure that you get all the rest that you need and keep your productivity levels up.

Your Assessment Skills

One of the most important skill sets that any instructor needs to have in their arsenal is their assessment skills. Obviously, they need these skills to be able to objectively evaluate their students' progress and performance, as well as their assignments, quizzes, and tests. There are several different kinds of assessment skills that instructors rely on to accomplish these. They are:

- Exam and quiz assessment techniques.

- "Classroom" assessment abilities.

- Intervention and interpretation skills.

Being able to accurately assess exams and quizzes requires that you know what exactly you are trying to evaluate in giving your students these quizzes and exams. In other words, it is knowing how to ask questions that can accurately gauge students' knowledge and progress. It's also looking at students' answers and being able to determine whether or not they fully reflect the knowledge or skills they are supposed to have learned.

"Classroom" assessment abilities, meanwhile, is your ability to evaluate how well your students are able to use the knowledge they are learning in class. Put simply, it is looking at student participation and in course-performance and being able to arrive at conclusions based on that.

Finally, intervention and interpretation skills are your ability to gauge how well students have understood a given concept, as well as determine what they've come to misunderstand or where they've made a mistake. In other words, it is being able to determine when you need to step in to correct a student's thinking or understanding.

To develop these various skill sets, instructors have to ask themselves certain questions. These questions can remind them of what exactly they are trying to measure or track in a student and help them see whether those students have been able to meet the learning objectives that have been set for them:

- What is my student supposed to get out of this assignment, quiz or test?

- How does this assignment align with the learning outcomes I want my student to achieve?

- What knowledge, skills, performance metric, or value am I trying to measure?

- How are the assignments that I have been giving out related to the quizzes and exams I have been giving or will be giving? Do the assignments properly prepare the students for these quizzes and tests?

- How are the different exams I give related to each other? Do they build on top of one another?

- What evaluation tactics, other than quizzes and exams, can I use to gauge student knowledge, skills, and performance?

- What kind of feedback have I been getting from my students and how can I use it to help my students improve?

Asking yourself such questions can both help you to evaluate your students' progress more thoroughly and adjust your teaching and evaluation methods. They can, for instance, help you to incorporate more evaluation methods into your course. This could be a great idea, seeing as not all students are good at taking tests, meaning that tests are not always a good indicator of their progress. Examples of these other kinds of evaluation methods might be surveys, portfolios, student presentations, and group projects. Having your students' complete assignments like these can help them demonstrate their knowledge far more than exams themselves can. They can show that your students really have learned and internalized what you were trying to teach them, rather than simply memorizing them and moving on.

Successful instructors typically are individuals who have worked to develop all these different skill sets before and even while launching their online courses. As a result, they have achieved staggering levels of success, just like you can. Achieving that success took a certain amount of time, of course, and in that time those instructors learned a lot. Given that, success stories are great examples to look to, as the experiences they went through can be quite instructive for you as well.

Checklist

	Set up an easy-to-use filing system
	Install premium virus protection and security software
	Brush up on computer skills and ensure you're familiar with presentation software and tools
	Create accounts for the appropriate video call software
	Create cloud-based backup for your lessons and assignments, as well as student submissions
	Ask your students for feedback
	Assess your assessment skills and continue to learn in order to improve the quality of your courses and the value your students receive

Chapter 8:
What Have I Learned As an Online Course Instructor?

While the online teaching industry started coming to more people's attention in 2020, it has been around for a good many years, as we have already seen. This means that there are many more success stories out there than you might have originally thought. It also means that some of the individuals that populate this industry and community have a decade or more years of experience under their belt. The experiences that these veterans of the online teaching world have gathered over the years and the insights that they have obtained through them are invaluable to their predecessors. This is doubly true for those instructors who are very new to online teaching. With that in mind, what can you learn from the veterans of the industry? What golden nuggets of information are contained in the stories they have to tell?

Michelle Leverson

Michelle Leverson first started teaching online courses in statistics in 2004, meaning nearly two decades ago. As such, she can be considered one of the first online instructors to venture into the space. In 2009, Leverson decided to pick up the pen and share some of the many different lessons she had learned through her unique journey, like the importance of open communication and how much of a difference it can make for students.

Open communication entails many things within the context of an online course. For instance, it entails letting students know that the instructor is there to actively help if and when they need it. It translates to getting back to students quickly—meaning within a promised time-frame—and creating safe discussion environments where students can feel free to take risks in. In short, it requires that you, as an instructor, have a strong presence online and thus, be accessible.

If you want to maintain a strong online presence, you can do so by letting students know when you will be reachable and through which channels. You can strengthen this presence and in fact, lay its very foundations by starting your courses with introductory videos, briefly explaining who you are. This way, you can humanize the very course that you are teaching, which can go a long way in community-building, as we have seen. You can even take this a step further and respond to your students' introductory videos, and make them feel really welcome in your "classroom." Keeping communication channels open like this is something that alleviates any hesitations that students might have to, say, ask questions, and for clarifications.

Another very important lesson that Leverson has learned is that students need a lot more extrinsic motivation in online courses than they would in physical ones. This is because, in a traditional classroom or workshop setting, students would get motivated by the physical presence of their instructor, the fact that everyone around them is working, and by the overall environment in general. Online courses typically lack these factors, which makes it hard for students who depend on them to find sources of motivation. Online instructors, then, have to put in added effort to be motivating for their students.

Despite what you may think, though, giving students the external motivation they need isn't exactly an arduous task. It just requires taking some very specific, though minor steps, like clearly specifying hard deadlines. By when do students need to turn in a certain assignment, if they want to complete your course? By what date and time do they need to finish watching a lesson that you already aired, if they want to keep going? Providing students with concrete deadlines like this can add fuel to their fire in a lot of cases. So can having students collaborate on different assignments projects, because then, they can become each other's source of external motivation. This makes an abundance of sense, once you consider how group projects and the like make people accountable to one another. That sense of accountability naturally increases their sense of discipline, responsibility, and, yes, motivation. Having students work together then isn't just a good community-building technique, but also a great motivational trick.

The same can be said about asking students for feedback. When students are asked their honest opinions regarding what works and what does not in a course, they feel heard, seen, and valued. What's more, they share perspectives, ideas, and observations you might not have considered before. Sometimes, though, sharing all these things with a course instructor directly can be slightly intimidating. At least that is what Levalle has observed. This is why she created chat groups in her online courses. These were groups that her students actively used to discuss anything and everything related to the course. Levalle herself seldom joined their conversation, but she did have full access to it. This means that she was able to tap into their unfiltered thoughts, opinions, and feelings directly. The students knew that Levalle could and would be watching the message boards, of course. It was not like their instructor was spying on them. But the option to discuss ways in which the course could be improved, without the potentially confrontational element that comes with talking directly with an instructor, was undoubtedly appreciated by them. Through observing what her students talked about, Levalle was able to get valid feedback and then use it to improve upon her course. Just as you can by keeping track of or moderating your student message boards or other chat systems.

Monash Faculty of Education Instructors

Levalle is naturally not the only instructor to gain important insight that she is ready and willing to share with prospective online instructors. The Monash Faculty of Education Instructors, who were forced to take to online teaching during the pandemic, do as well. Admittedly, these instructors' initial experience was a little different than Levalle's. After all, unlike her, they were pushed toward a teaching model that they hadn't considered before, by global circumstances. What these instructors quickly came to find out though, is that they—and you— could do several things to improve student–instructor relationships, keep building communities within their classrooms and turn online teaching into a highly sustainable system. The group would list their hard-earned insights as follows:

- **Humanize the online teaching experience**. It's easy to forget that you are dealing with real-life people, be they students or teachers, where online courses are concerned. This is to be expected, given how removed from physical interactions online teaching can be. This is precisely why instructors need to strive to humanize the teaching process. This does not just mean reaching out to students and working on building relationships with them. It means working personal touches, like life experiences and lived anecdotes, into their lessons and lectures. Doing this is a very simple way of taking what students are learning and turning it from some abstract concept into a personal, relevant story that they can engage with and be impacted by. The great thing about these methods is that they can be further expanded on during in-course discussions and reflections. Students can ask questions about these stories, debate various aspects of them, and even share similar or contrasting stories of their own. Through this process, they can start linking the experiences of different individuals, while revisiting the very things they learned within them.

- **Attend to your students' emotions**. Your students' emotional needs and reactions are a vital part of any course, be it in person or virtual. Attending to your students' emotions is important, because it can help and allow you to create a safe, virtual space. This is something that the Monash Faculty discovered after they started picking up on how the COVID-19 pandemic impacted their students' mental well-being. Arriving at this realization prompted the Monash Faculty to pay greater attention to their students' emotional world and try to provide them with a space where they could discuss them more. Once students had a safe space to begin exploring how they felt, once they saw that they could express their feelings and be heard, the burden of their struggles began to lessen. As a result, their overall performance in their courses improved, and so did their grades and the quality of their interactions with one another.

- **Bring your personality to the virtual space you are in**. One of the things the Monash Faculty struggled the most with is how to incorporate their own personalities into their courses, now that they could not physically be in them. After all, talking to a video camera or even Zoom chat box does not feel like a very personal or human experience. So, it can make letting your personality shine through difficult, to say the least. One way that the faculty members found to overcome this hurdle is to create their assignments and video tutorials from scratch, rather than using pre-made assignments or following scripts that were written for them. While there is nothing wrong with finding good, free-to-use assignments online, creating your own, unique examples is essential, if you want to bring your personality into your lessons. The same is true for your writing your own video scripts and lectures. Relying on the work of others for these purposes might save you some time, but it will also become a barrier to you connecting with your students. This is something that online instructors must avoid, if they want to achieve the kind of success that they dream of achieving.

Checklist

	Humanize the teaching experience
	Validate your students' emotions
	Personalize your classes

Conclusion

As you have seen throughout the vast majority of *Online Course Mastery: The Ultimate Guide to Creating and Marketing Profitable Online Courses*, starting an online course might be one of the best things that you do for yourself. The prime reason for this is that online courses, if done well, can very easily become a passive income source for you. A good online course works a bit like a windmill. Yes, you'll have to put plenty of time and effort into building your windmill. However, once you have the steadily blowing breeze, it will keep the windmill running. You might have to do some maintenance work over the years and update the mill here and there. But beyond that, you won't have to put in any heavy work to keep this thing that you produced operational. At least, not until you decide to launch another online course.

Naturally, ensuring that your online course functions in perpetuity in this way requires a considerable amount of thought and energy. To start, you'll have to find the right online course to teach. Ideally, this will be something that combines your passion, interest, and expertise, something that you can confidently teach others about. To accomplish this, you'll have to figure out what your passions and interests are by asking yourself certain questions, like "What kind of problems am I able to solve?" and "What topics and subtopics do I enjoy learning about the most?"

Once you have nailed down your interests, skills, and passions, you'll need to consider your target audience and their needs carefully. You'll need to find the Venn diagram where these two things coincide and build your course right there. To really make sure that your course is a success, you'll have to do some market research too.

Having identified your niche and understood your market, with all its details and intricacies, the real work of building your course will begin. The first step you need to take, in this regard, is to create your very own syllabus. Your syllabus will be the guide to structuring your course. It'll also be the guide that your students use to navigate it. A good syllabus will consist of things like a clear course description and a well-laid out course schedule, but it also takes your learning goal into careful consideration. Your learning goal will play an even bigger role in determining your learning objectives, which you will utilize to devise your lesson plans and create your course materials.

Once you've created a solid syllabus and lesson plans, you'll be able to move on to considering which online teaching platform you want to use. There are several platforms that you can use, such as Teachable, Podia, Thinkific, Kajabi, LearnDash, and Udemy. Each and every one of these platforms come with their own set of advantages and challenges. You will need to give careful consideration to these, as well as to your needs, wants, strengths, and weaknesses if you want to choose the best one for you. Remember: there will not be a universally right answer to give in this regard. There will only be a right answer for *you*.

After choosing your platform and creating an account on it, you'll be able to start uploading your course material on it. But of course, this requires having course materials to upload to begin with. Your course materials will be things like the video tutorials that make up your lessons, written texts, PowerPoint presentations, course assignments, quizzes, and tests. Creating each of these things will be a process and need to be a well-thought out one at that. You'll have to always bear your audience and their needs in mind as you create your content and strive to meet them. This will entail doing all sorts of things like writing scripts for your videos, doing storyboards for them and your presentations, adding interactive elements to YouTube videos... Essentially, it will entail making the process of learning as interactive and engaging as possible for your students.

The process of creation won't end there, because next up will be the actual filming and editing portion. Thankfully, you won't need to be technologically gifted to be able to film and edit the videos you prepare for your class. You won't even really have to be technologically literate. All you'll have to do is download the right software and know which buttons to click and voila! You'll have the perfect, good-quality videos you want. You'll have to approach creating your assignments with the same diligence and gusto that you show in creating your course videos. You'll have to follow certain rules in creating them too, like taking care to always be crystal clear and dividing big assignments into smaller ones. You'll obviously have to decide on which assignments you want to hand out before you go about handing them out. But luckily, you'll have an array of options to choose from, like presentations, collaborative worksheets, group projects, mind and concept maps, to name a few.

After you've created your online "school" on your chosen platform and created and uploaded all the course materials you need for it, you'll move on to the glorious work of marketing. After all, creating the best course in the world won't achieve much of anything if no one knows that the course exists. You have to get the word out about it somehow and you do that through online marketing and social media marketing. To that end, you'll be able to make use of many, many different strategies. Determining which strategies to turn to will begin with creating your marketing plan. Your marketing plan will be your guide to the marketing process, just as your syllabus was your guide to creating and navigating your course. In creating your marketing plan, you'll have to consider important factors like your value proposition, key performance indicators, target market, and budget. Then, you'll use these factors to determine which strategies are the best ones for you to follow. The online marketing strategies you opt for can be anything from creating a good landing page to publishing an eBook, making use of SEO and content marketing, and to working with other instructors. Meanwhile, your social media marketing strategies can range from creating a good promo video to starting a YouTube channel and regularly engaging with your social media communities.

This latter will be particularly important for you, by virtue of how important communities are for online courses. Building a community is an absolute must, after all, if you want to have the kind of online course that generates an income for you years and years after it has been created. This is because community building is a great way of spreading the word about your course. It's also because communities are known for supporting their members—which include you and your students—and are great for learning environments. Learning from your community effectively means gaining insight that you can then use to make improvements to your course and take it to newfound heights.

Being able to achieve all this is contingent on being able to build a community around your online course. You can easily do this, though, so long as you prioritize clear, two-way communication between you and your students. This means checking in with your students, providing them with avenues to contact and keep in touch with you, as well as with each other. It further means asking for feedback from students and then taking what you discover to strengthen your lessons. Aside from this, building a strong social presence, thereby giving your students a sense of immediacy and intimacy are also vital for the longevity and integrity of your course. Without this, the course you create cannot sustain itself for long.

An added benefit of building a community around your course is that it can help you to overcome some common hurdles that often stop students from either participating in or continuing with their online education. From technological hurdles to resistance to change, a lack of interactivity to a lack of motivation, these can all be massive problems for students. However, they're all easy-to-overcome issues as well, so long as you employ solutions that address their root causes.

Being able to achieve this, however, requires that you either have or work to polish certain skill sets. As an online instructor, you will heavily rely on four different skill sets. These are your technical skills, interpersonal skills, time management and organizational skills, and assessment skills. An instructor who is able to master all four different types of skills will not only draw more and more students to their courses on a regular basis, but also get their students to really emotionally invest in what they are learning. These are the instructors that can truly infuse their students with a sense that they've found a community that they belong in and are learning something worthwhile.

The technical skills you need to master will be relatively simple ones, like knowing how to manage and organize your files and using video chatting and communication tools. Your interpersonal, time management, and organizational and assessment skills, though, may take a bit more time and effort to master. As a quick recap, your interpersonal skills mean your empathic abilities, along with your communication skills, patience, ability to actively listen to others, give positive reinforcement, and your levels of self-confidence. Your time management and organizational skills, meanwhile, have to do with how well you're able to manage your time, prioritize your to-dos, and split them across your schedule. Your assessment skills, on the other hand, are both your ability to create assignments, quizzes and tests that can accurately measure your students' progress and objectively interpret what the results of those assignments are telling you.

Developing all these skills might initially sound challenging and overwhelming. Luckily, by adopting the various strategies and techniques outlined in *A Complete Guide to Creating Online Courses*, you'll be able to accomplish all this and more. For instance, strategies like asking your students open-ended questions can go a long way to develop your empathic abilities and active listening skills. So can validating your students' feelings and using "I feel" statements when you can. Meanwhile, techniques like considering which of your to-dos are priorities based on their deadlines and level of importance can help you stick to a work schedule that works for you. Making sure that you schedule in breaks, on the other hand, can ensure that you keep that schedule realistic by giving your mind and body the time it needs to rest and recuperate. While this strategy may sound counterintuitive to some, it's actually something that can rejuvenate you a great deal, and increase your performance as an online course instructor and thus the quality of the work that you do.

The better the quality of your work, the more students will be drawn to it. The more communicative and empathic you are, the better a connection you will forge with your students. The stronger your connections with your students, the more robust and larger the community you build around your course will be. This is just one small reason why working on your various skills and improving upon them is a must if you want to keep your online course going. The funny thing is, once you start making a dedicated effort to achieve this, you'll be surprised at how quickly you will improve your skill set and how rapidly your online course following will grow. It really should not be, though. After all, it is very understandable that your students would see and appreciate the devotion that you show to them and the efforts you go to accommodate them and respond to this situation with genuine enthusiasm. It is this kind of genuine effort that is bound to turn your students into your very own brand ambassadors who freely and happily spread the word about the amazing work you are doing, after all.

Now that you know all that you need to know to discover your subject, create your course, and market it as it deserves to be marketed, you have all that you need to make it a resounding success. In other words, you have all that you need to go out there and start putting what you have learned to good use. The only question you have to answer, then, is this: what are you still waiting for?

Thank you for reading *Online Course Mastery: The Ultimate Guide to Creating and Marketing Profitable Online Courses*. We hope that you enjoyed reading it. If you have enjoyed the read and found it to be useful, please leave a review!

Before you go, we just wanted to say thank you for purchasing our book. You could have picked from dozens of other books on the same topic but you took a chance and chose this one. So, a HUGE thanks to you for getting this book and for reading all the way to the end.

Now, we wanted to ask you for a small favor. COULD YOU PLEASE CONSIDER POSTING A REVIEW ON THE PLATFORM? (Reviews are one of the easiest ways to support the work of independent authors.)

This feedback will help us continue to write the type of books that will help you get the results you want. So if you enjoyed it, please let us know!

We wish you much Success on your Journey!

Made in United States
Troutdale, OR
08/11/2025

33555669R00086